BRAND *IS* DESTINY

The Ultimate Bottom Line

Also by Marc Rudov

*Be Unique or Be Ignored: The CEO's
Guide to Branding*

BRAND *IS* DESTINY

The Ultimate Bottom Line

MARC RUDOV

MHR Enterprises

MHR Enterprises

Brand Is Destiny
The Ultimate Bottom Line

By Marc H. Rudov

Published by:
MHR Enterprises
MarcRudov.com

ISBN: 978-0-9745017-4-1 (paperback)
ISBN: 978-0-9745017-6-5 (eBook)

Library of Congress Data
Rudov, Marc H.,
    Brand is destiny: the ultimate bottom line/Marc H. Rudov
    —1st ed.
    ISBN: **978-0-9745017-4-1** (paperback)
    1. Branding
    2. Marketing
    3. Sales
    4. Business strategy
    5. Management

Library of Congress Control Number: 2016919568

Control your own destiny or someone else will.

Jack Welch
Former CEO of General Electric

DEDICATION

To Galileo Galilei—astronomer, mathematician, philosopher, and scientist—who shaped mankind's destiny, risking his reputation, freedom, and life, by espousing the heretical, politically incorrect, but *accurate*, astronomical model of heliocentrism (Earth revolves around the Sun).

The Catholic Church embraced geocentrism (the Sun revolves around Earth). In 1633, Pope Urban VIII ordered Galileo to be placed under house arrest, which lasted until he died in 1642.

Table of Contents

PREFACE

If you want to watch a sunset, you'd better be heading west. Direction and destiny are mutually dependent.

This book explains how and why a brand establishes your company's purpose and direction—*and is, therefore, its destiny and ultimate bottom line.*

An old college friend recently joined the board of a young biotech company. Prior to his first board meeting, we had discussed the prospect of me providing branding counsel to the CEO. He promised to put me on that meeting's agenda.

After the board meeting, he sent me this predictable text message: "No interest at this time, Marc. Will keep you in mind when we launch the product in 12-18 months."

The time for branding is **before** *conceiving the product,* not at the time of launching it, a year-and-a-half hence—when branding will become a clunky shoehorning exercise.

This tale, sadly, is common. It epitomizes acutely the typical CEO's paltry grasp of and regard for branding; and depicts why most firms' brands—*unique, customer-validated value propositions*—are impotent, invisible, or repellent.

Most CEOs believe that branding is akin to painting: a task one executes *after* building a structure. Wrong. Others confuse it with public relations (PR). Wrong again. In fact, the brand is the *foundation:* Who builds a foundation last?

It turns out that, in the business world, plenty of board-enabled execs attempt to do exactly that.

In *Be Unique or Be Ignored,* my prior book, I asserted that, despite the paucity of chief executives and their boards of directors understanding or valuing branding, it *is* their #1 priority: *it must precede all else.* Can you spell disconnect?

What have I discovered since publishing that book? The picture is much worse than I ever had imagined: CEOs are downright *dismissive* of branding.

People dismiss attitudes and endeavors unfamiliar and uncomfortable to them, especially those that differ from what their compatriots embrace. In addition to outright disdain and trivialization, here are five reasons CEOs dismiss branding:

- Fear of isolation, being unique, and standing out
- Overreliance on phony, detached social media
- Obsession with acquiring the latest technology
- Preoccupation with disruption
- Fear of offending politically correct Millennials and their "adult" imitators and enablers.

Contrary to the conventional belief, a strong, effective brand—*not* a cool product—generates the best route to a great destiny: sustainable customer loyalty and profitability.

Paraphrasing Lewis Carroll, *If you don't know where you're going, any product will get you there.* Regrettably, too many companies, ricocheting randomly like pinballs in their competitive domains, follow this product-centric recipe.

You must, therefore, determine where you're going—control your company's destiny—*before* leaving the dock. Or else, as Jack Welch, former CEO of General Electric, used to warn his employees, *someone else will.*

Never confuse destiny with destination. Destiny is a path, a route, a vector. Destination, on the other hand, is a stopping point. Successful firms never stop; they keep moving forward in sustainably profitable directions.

Think of your brand as the coordinates you enter into a GPS. If saddled with a nebulous brand (doesn't resonate with customers), your enterprise will drift haphazardly like an aimless ship. An atrocious brand (repels customers), will crash your vessel into an iceberg. Think Titanic.

In short, that is why brand is destiny, the ultimate bottom line. Pretending otherwise is futile and expensive.

Finally, CEOs, executives at all levels, and boards of directors must connect brand, destiny, and bottom line. It is an immutable connection, which, if respected, will beget great, enduring business success.

MARC H. RUDOV
February 2017
Bay Area, CA

CHAPTER ONE

Branding Review

Vince Lombardi, legendary coach of the NFL's Green Bay Packers during the '60s, gathered his players at the start of each season, football in hand, to review game fundamentals and reiterate team objectives: "Gentlemen, this is a football."

Even though "Branding Basics" is the first chapter of my prior book, *Be Unique or Be Ignored: The CEO's Guide to Branding,* reviewing the salient concepts here will benefit you.

Likewise, if you and your employees currently misuse brand and branding, akin to misusing market and marketing, absorbing the axioms of this and my prior book is essential.

What a Brand Is and Isn't

A brand is a *customer-validated value proposition.* It is intangible but vital. One expresses the brand, verbally and in writing, in *customer language:* it originates with customers. That means *no* vendor or industry jargon, and *no* mention of products, services, and technologies. **Most critical:** Your company must walk its talk: ***deliver the brand's promise.***

Because the brand establishes a company's purpose and direction, branding is the CEO's #1 priority, as the cost of *not* sticking the target—traveling toward the chosen destiny—kills the bottom line.

In contrast to your current belief, branding **precedes** products, customers, and revenues. Every time a customer, investor, or reporter asks you to repeat, once again, what your company offers, you know your brand has failed.

In addition, a brand is *not* a logo; a logo is *not* a brand. The logo, a graphical symbol, *represents* a brand but never *constitutes* one. So, if you just hired a design agency to create a new logo and label, that's all you have. *Never* announce that your old logo *was* your brand and new logo *is* your brand.

Moreover, many professionals in business and media circles blithely *but mistakenly* refer to company and product names, and labels and SKUs, as brands. **Unless customers are *emotionally connected* to a company name or product name, it's just a *word*—and that's true in most cases.**

What Is a Brand?

N⊘T a logo, label, or SKU

N⊘T a product name

N⊘T a product description

N⊘T a company name

N⊘T a company description

© 2017 MarcRudov.com

Example: The Upscale Beauty Spa

Picture an upscale beauty spa. The brand of this spa is: *We keep you feeling young, beautiful, and confident.* Why *this* brand? Because it encapsulates customer desires, *in their language.* Notice what's missing: product, service, and jargon. Ultimately, the spa *must* walk the talk (promise) of its brand.

Now imagine a woman making her periodic pilgrimage to this spa. She visits her regular beautician, who urges her to purchase the latest-and-greatest skin cream. She does so.

Why? She *wants* to keep feeling young, beautiful, and confident. Based on previous experiences with this spa, this customer trusts implicitly her vendor's recommendations.

Finally, the customer returns three weeks later to see her beautician, who asks about the skin cream's results. Our customer is ecstatic. To her surprise, though, the beautician announces that she's discovered an even-better product and implored her to purchase it, which she did. Strong brand.

What has changed in three weeks? The product. What has *not* changed in three weeks? The brand. That's how *real* branding looks and works. Strong brands endure.

If your reaction to my spa example is that it doesn't apply because your company is in the industrial, commercial, technology, scientific, healthcare, or military world, you are misinformed. Buckle up for an education and transformation.

Branding applies to *all* industries and customers. Every customer in every sector is a human being who buys with emotion (see the GutShare section below). It's just that consumer examples are universally understood.

Because the goal of branding is to establish a gut-level connection with customers, investors, employees, and other stakeholders, it is mandatory in *all* business sectors, without exception, regardless of company size or age.

The strongest brand *always* wins. The strongest product, however, *does not.* Even if a hot product wins in the short term, it can't sustain a company's profitability, growth, and customer loyalty and trust in the long term. Dismissing this truth, therefore, is unwise and will lead to failure.

Brand Outranks You

You stare out the window, proud of the view from your corner office, reflecting on your climb to this lofty perch.

Newsflash: Customers don't care about you, your rank, your perch, or your perks.

It's amazing how myopically smug executives and employees can become over time. They obsess over their org charts, processes, products, solar panels, and beer blasts.

Warning: Internal focus and smugness can ruin any company, at any stage of its life.

I've had this exchange multiple times with so-called "customer service" reps in large and small companies alike; I'll bet you can relate:

Rudov: There's an error in my invoice.

CS Rep: Let me explain how our company works.

Rudov: I don't care how your company works. It's irrelevant to me. Your job is to help me, *despite* your internal structure.

This is a classical example of what I call an *entroprise*, a chaotic enterprise, a rudderless corporation without any obvious reason to exist, other than to impress its competitors and fool its shareholders. Talk to the rank-and-file: they're just hoping the paychecks and health insurance won't end.

In October 2015, in the largest tech deal ever, at the time, Dell Inc. acquired EMC Corporation for $67B. Layoffs ensued. Michael Dell, CEO of this private behemoth, now called Dell Technologies, explained the acquisition with financial-speak and formulaic bloviating about technological synergies. Not once, however, did Mr. Dell mention *customers* of either entity, or how this merger will benefit them.

Reality: the Dell-EMC combination won't and can't work, regardless of how cool it appears on paper, if it doesn't offer a unique brand to an identifiable market.

Similarly, in January 2016, famed investor Carl Icahn forced brandless, undervalued Xerox to split in two. Ironically, Ursula Burns, CEO of Xerox, had purchased Dallas–based Affiliated Computer Services (ACS) for $6 billion in 2010, to mask her company's weak brand. Because of Icahn, she had to spin off ACS into a new company called, drum-roll, please, Conduent. Xerox is back to copiers and printing.

If you've deduced a recurring theme here, you're right. In fact, this theme pervades the business world.

The brand is the true CEO of your enterprise: *every employee, process, and product reports to it.* The CEO, like the brand, sets the company's direction and purpose.

Brand Outranks You

BRAND

PEOPLE **PROCESSES** **PRODUCTS**

© 2016 MarcRudov.com

With a weak CEO, as with a weak brand, there's total chaos—and bloated costs of sales, capital, and media.

Bottom line: the brand outranks you and everything else in your company. It is the reason your company exists. The brand determines both the kind of people, processes, and products that are required—and superfluous.

Until proving to those directly and indirectly attached to your firm that brand rules people, processes, and products, you'll operate suboptimally and haphazardly—pleasing your competitors and angering your shareholders.

Brand Essentials

Think back to the brand of our mythical beauty spa: *We keep you feeling young, beautiful, and confident.*

Why would it please customers? Trust. It defines them, *in their language.* It reflects their desires. It's unique, succinct, and pithy. They' *react* to it, *remember* it, and *repeat* it.

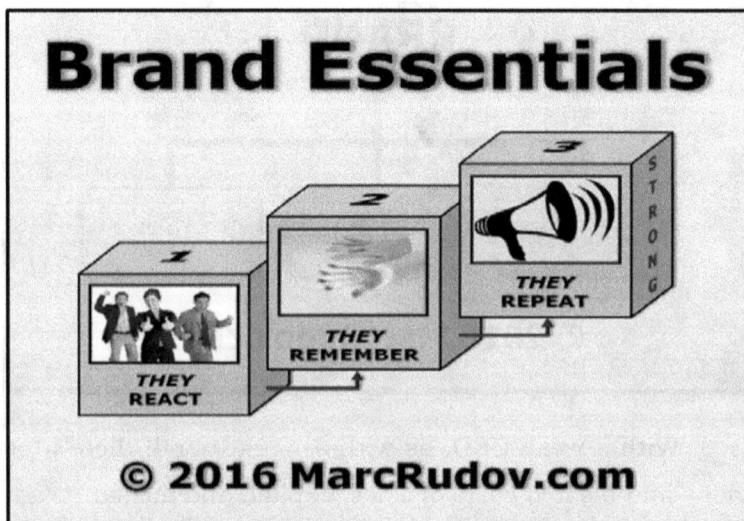

If people don't react viscerally to your brand—*meaning there must be an emotional component*—they won't remember it. If they can't remember it, they won't repeat it. If they don't repeat it, there will be no word of mouth. This is failure.

Your company, regardless of industry, size, age, or geography, must respect and employ these brand essentials. If, however, success is unimportant to you, your team, and your board of directors, ignore what you just read.

Five Stages of Branding

I've discovered that, similar to the process of grieving, branding occurs in five stages. Let me make it clear: It *shouldn't* be this way, but too often it *is* this way—because so many CEOs dismiss and resist it.

Five Stages of Branding

DENIAL
We're not ready. Did it last year. Not a priority.

ANGER
Spent $$ on ads. Liked on social sites. Few customers.

NEGOTIATION
If we use more, newer jargon, will we get respect?

DEPRESSION
We're still in the white noise. My staff is demoralized.

ACCEPTANCE
OK, we have no brand. Maybe we should create one.

© 2017 MarcRudov.com

You doubt me? How many suppliers in your industry look and sound the same, use the same jargon, hire the same people, make the same claims at conferences and in white papers, and believe new technologies and products magically will propel them to success? Perhaps your company is guilty.

GoPro, the once-vaunted supplier of wearable action cameras, comes to mind. In 2014, its stock peaked at $87. In November 2016, to become profitable, the firm laid off 15 percent of its 1500 employees and closed its entertainment division. Its stock was around $10. Despite all the hoopla and attention, GoPro never had a brand—only products.

Any CEO who claims, "We're not ready for branding. We did it last year. It's not a priority," is in denial and hurting her company. Imagine Andy Murray, currently the world's #1 pro tennis player, arrogantly bragging, "I improved myself last year and am not ready to do it again. It's not a priority."

Branding not only *precedes* products, customers, and revenues, it is a continuous, top-priority process. Skip to the *acceptance stage*, stay there, and never look back.

What Is Unique?

As you learned in my previous book, your corporate brand is unique, weak, or nonexistent. If nonexistent, your firm appears to the outside world as a generic producer of commodities, in which case your competitive advantage is embodied in price, delivery, or both.

On the other hand, business vastly improves with a unique brand. Customers emotionally connect with it, can choose it easily from a bevy of competitors, and ***willingly pay a premium for your product or service***.

Notice that I distinguished brand from product. You must do likewise when envisioning, planning, and embarking on your company's journey to destiny.

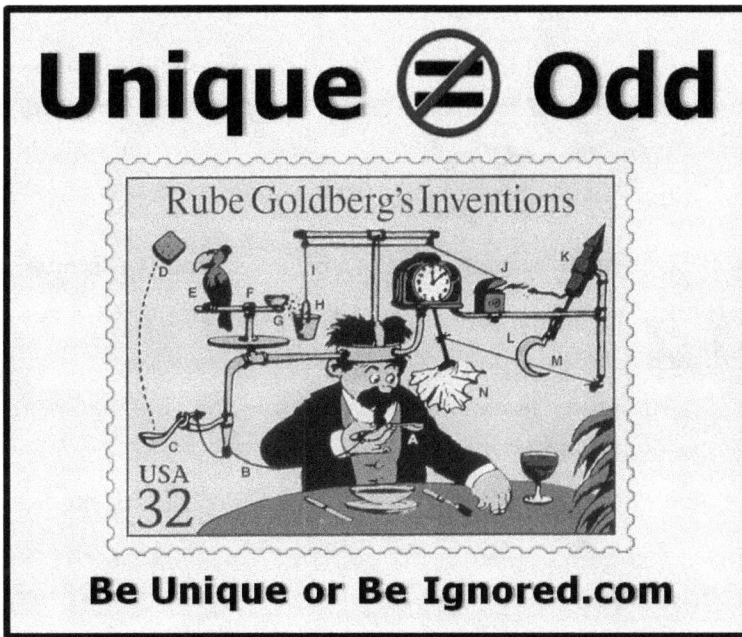

Rube Goldberg's Inventions
USA 32
Unique ≠ Odd
Be Unique or Be Ignored.com

Never misconstrue or misuse "unique." Unique is not veneer. It does not mean weird, odd (Rube Goldberg device), or unusual in color or shape. Unique—*one of a kind*—pertains to singular *value*, as customers define it, articulated as they like to hear and read it (see the spa example above).

As I explain in *Be Unique or Be Ignored*, suppliers in all industries tend to imitate each other—preferring blending over branding, jargon over customer lingo, presumption over explanation, ambiguity over clarity.

Mark Leibovich's provocative page-turner, *This Town*, about the inner-workings of Washington, DC, aptly explains this pervasive blending/ambiguity phenomenon:

> *"You know you've made it in DC when someone says that—'It isn't clear what he does'—about you. Such people used to have such an air of mystery about them. You assumed they did something exotic, like work for the CIA ... Ambiguity pays well here."*

Leibovich is claiming that *brand* in politics is elusive, irrelevant, and/or undesirable, that being unique is a recipe for disaster. False. Donald Trump broke this mold.

Ambiguity is expensive. It's ironic that business execs simultaneously hate *and* emulate politicians, who don't care: they spend *our* money. *You spend your shareholders' money.*

Jargon Squeezes Margin

You may think me a broken record for railing against jargon. Too bad. I won't stop. It is injurious to your business.

When people want to communicate only to a small circle—for secrecy, exclusivity, snobbery, or brevity—they use jargon, vernacular, buzzwords. Knowing and speaking jargon, they believe, confers special *insider* status upon them.

If you happen upon two members of any industry, regardless of venue, they'll be engaged in an indecipherable jargonfest known as "inside baseball." William Safire, who for years penned the *New York Times Magazine's* "On Language" column, wrote a piece in 1988 called "Inside Baseball," which he defined as *minutiae savored by the cognoscenti, delicious details, nuances discussed and dissected by aficionados.*

This is a disaster in the making! Why?

1. Jargon is *not* customer language and, therefore, antithetical to building a strong brand

2. Jargon is *generic.* Jargon is salesforce camouflage. Generic means commodity, the opposite of unique, the bane of high profit margins

3. Jargon is ambrosia to the lazy, untalented, risk-averse, club-minded hacks: nobody ever got fired for using it; that's why it's so annoyingly pervasive.

But, here's the conflict: branding requires boldness, creativity (not imitation), knowledge of and bias toward customers, and the willingness, courage, and desire to stand alone. Few people in business circles, let alone the general population, are equipped with these required qualities.

I once pitched my branding services to a PhD-educated CEO of a startup tech company in Silicon Valley. He told me that learning to communicate plainly had been a tough adjustment. Academic elitists, at universities and prestigious journals, view clear-speaking/writing PhDs with derision and disdain, and will not publish their works.

Jargon Button

lazy

Be Unique or Be Ignored.com

Translation: prestige and fathomability are inversely proportional in ivory (and ivy) towers.

It takes desire and effort to understand the language of your customers. Yet, you're too busy spewing jargon (I saw your homepage). You believe that customers understand and like your jargon—*or that you can force them to use it*—because it's so obviously superior to their plain, everyday language.

Newsflash: Vendors that can't or don't or won't speak in customer lingo are taking the lazy way out: they are hitting the jargon button, thereby raising the costs of sales, capital, and media. Jargonistas have no place in branding.

The more company meetings and industry conferences you attend, the more jargon you will hear and spread. Most assuredly, you'll teach your employees, PR firms, and ad agencies to perpetuate it. Finally, you *will* reinforce the cachet of insider status and become increasingly disconnected from the outside world.

Microsoft runs TV spots to promote its "cloud" service. Cloud is a meaningless term. *There is no cloud.* Cloud is the new Kleenex: generic. Here's the script from a March, 2016, spot, with the voiceover (VO) and two executives from Geneva-based Temenos, a maker of banking software:

VO: Right now, there are two billion people who don't have access to basic banking. But, that is changing.

Ben Robinson: At Temenos, we use the Microsoft Cloud to provide banking to the millions and millions of people who need it but don't have access to it. With the Microsoft Cloud, we can enable a banker to travel to the most remote locations with nothing but a phone and a tablet.

Murray Gardiner: More and more people are getting access to credit. Everywhere where there's a phone, you have a bank. So, now a person is able to start a business and generate an income and employ somebody for the first time. And, you can actually see the success. It's transforming our world.

Ben Robinson: The Microsoft Cloud helped us to bring banking to 10-million people in just two years. That's potentially 10-million new businesses.

VO: Technology is about breaking down barriers, removing limitations, so that every person has access to opportunity.

Ben Robinson: The small amount of money can change people's lives. It's very, very powerful.

At fadeout, we see a graphic displaying the Microsoft logo, the word Microsoft next to the meaningless, generic word "Cloud," followed by the tagline, *Empowering Business.*

Microsoft literally negates its brand by using jargon in its service name. Unsurprisingly, all of its competitors, such as IBM and Oracle, use it, too. Laziness in the extreme.

Put yourself in the viewer's chair. You're seeing a need for banking in remote geographies. Check. Microsoft and its partner Temenos have a solution. Check. Is it unique? Nope. Do you feel a connection? Nope. Branding blunder.

This common blunder, unfortunately, occurs daily in every company that does not make branding its #1 priority.

Return to the script. Replace "the Microsoft Cloud" with just Microsoft. Sounds and feels totally different, and much better, doesn't it? Better yet, replace it with a unique moniker, say Geo. *Microsoft Geo.* I'm not claiming this is the best choice but am illustrating my point: *Microsoft Geo helped us to bring banking to 10 million people in two years.* Bingo.

Finally, jargon squeezes margin. By genericizing your product, thereby eliminating its cache, you'll simultaneously reduce its price (no premium for commodities) and increase its cost of sales (harder to sell vis-à-vis lookalike products).

As the CEO and brander-in-chief, you must forbid the laziness of jargon—starting within yourself. Attain *outsider* status: what customers, investors, and reporters expect and will appreciate. Destroy your company's jargon button today.

GutShare™

Teach this to all of your employees: *People do not make cerebral decisions. They make gut decisions, a combination of logical and emotional. So, we'll cease making cerebral pitches through all of our megaphones.*

Then, you must enforce it, and that will be difficult and countercultural. But, you must enforce it.

The gold is in the gut, and your brand is the key to unlocking it—and profits. Yet, your firm likely is pitching facts via your salesreps, ads, PR, brochures, homepage, and speeches—because you believe in the myth of mindshare.

In fact, the typical corporate homepage reads like a nutritional label, imitating the homepages of all competitors in its industry: 100% factual, generic, **0% GutShare**. People feel safe spewing jargon and "fitting in." Boring and ineffective.

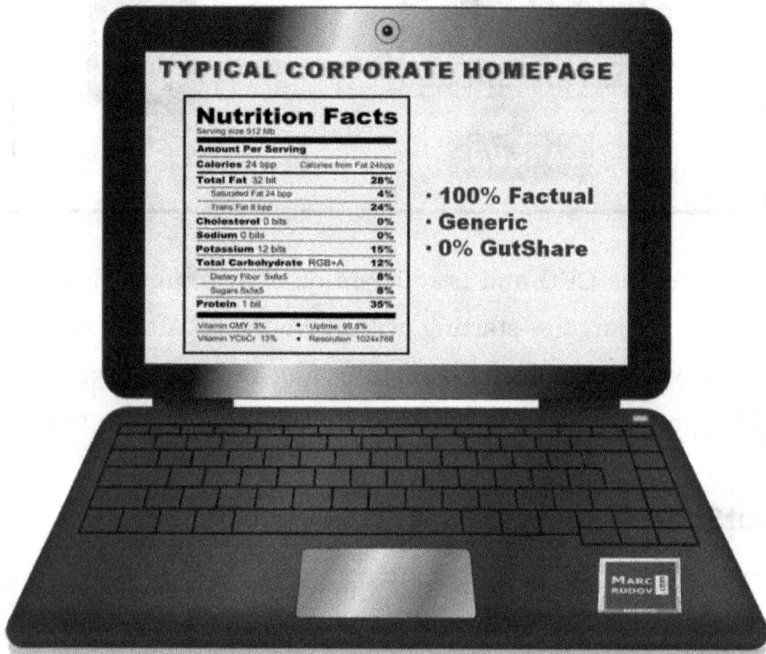

Only those who've never engaged in face-to-face selling and negotiating have trouble grasping GutShare. Worse, they don't comprehend the concept of corporate emotions.

I've heard this maddening bullshit, ad nauseam, for years: *Business executives make logical decisions, so branding is irrelevant in B2B situations. Only consumers make emotional purchases.* This is wrong, wrong, wrong.

Nobody, including you, makes purely logical decisions, ever, in any realm of life. *Every* decision in the business world, including whom to invite to a meeting, has a strong emotional component. Ignore this fact at your peril.

There are three universal corporate emotions: ***power, reputation, and paycheck***. Your brand, and by extension your salespitch, *must* reflect the emotions specific to your customers (market). Consider what's at stake when your customers put their asses on the line to purchase from you.

CORPORATE EMOTIONS
Foundation of GutShare

Power

Reputation

Paycheck

WHAT ARE THEY SAYING ABOUT YOU?

LENDER FORECLOSURE HOME AUCTION!

OPEN HOUSE
5/6, 5/12, 5/13

GutShare.com

Committees Kill Brands

In *Be Unique or Be Ignored*, I discussed the deleterious effect of committees on branding, in the "Politics in Branding" chapter. In addition, I explored it in subsequent articles and videos (MarcRudov.TV). This topic could itself fill a book.

Typically, if someone doesn't know what he's doing, in any endeavor, he first forms a committee to "study" it.

Also, under the guise of political correctness, there's a belief that getting everybody's opinion and treating it as equal in weight, yields superior results and satisfies all.

Alas, no committee, anywhere, ever produced anything creative and bold. Instead, the output of committees is diluted pablum, at best. Brands are no exceptions.

Artist Andy Warhol posited a brilliant branding axiom: "The moment you label something, you take a step. I mean, you can never go back again to seeing it unlabeled."

People fear taking that step, going alone out on a limb. They feel safer hiding in a feckless committee. That way, no one person gets blamed for a failure.

And, nobody will get credit for a spectacular success, either—because there won't be one.

Think of any iconic building in the world: The White House, Eiffel Tower, One World Trade Center in New York City, Guggenheim Museum in Bilbao, Sydney Opera House. A principal architect, *not a committee*, designed it.

Gap Inc., the clothing-retailer holding company, is now in a rut—with its Gap and Banana Republic chains leading the downward trajectory. It has experienced seven straight quarters of lower sales.

Now, the retailer is experiencing an internal struggle—to be centralized vs. decentralized, to use creative directors or branding committees—over how best to right the flagging firm.

Here are three revealing comments about Gap Inc., as reported on 11/28/16 in the *Wall Street Journal*:

> Garrett Bennett, retail consultant at Merchandising Metrics: *"You knew what Gap stood for when Mickey Drexler was running it. When you don't have a creative visionary leading a company, you can't really establish a consistent look over a period of time and reinforce the brand's purpose."*

Wendi Goldman, chief product officer for the Gap brand: *"[CEO] Mr. Peck's new approach is about taking out the voice of one creative head and allowing a creative ecosystem to exist."*

Todd Oldham, a former creative director at Old Navy: *"Anything that has to become a consensus is an equation for dilution. Without a distinct point of view, you become like everyone else."*

What comes across in these Gap quotes? Which words and phrases jump out? I see: *consensus, creative ecosystem, dilution, no distinct point of view, no purpose, risk-aversion, imitation, become like everyone else.* **Committees kill brands**.

Bottom Line

Vice President Joe Biden shrewdly deduced this about the basis for Hillary Clinton's 2016 presidential bid: "I don't think she ever really figured it out." Spot-on observation.

In fact, she spent *two years* with committees and focus groups, trying to figure it out but didn't. She's like Yahoo and Twitter, neither of which can articulate why it exists.

Despite her name-and fame, Hillary Clinton spent $1.2B (Trump spent half that), had no brand, and dismissed and dissed America's "deplorable" core: the middle class.

Lesson: Defective brand begets deadly destiny, which yields disastrous bottom line. Never forget this!

CHAPTER TWO

Market Review

Many words in the business lexicon are misused and incorrectly interchanged, but none more so than *market*. I covered this in *Be Unique or Be Ignored*, but review is needed.

Let's look at fishing. The root of fishing is *fish*. Nobody on this planet would argue with that.

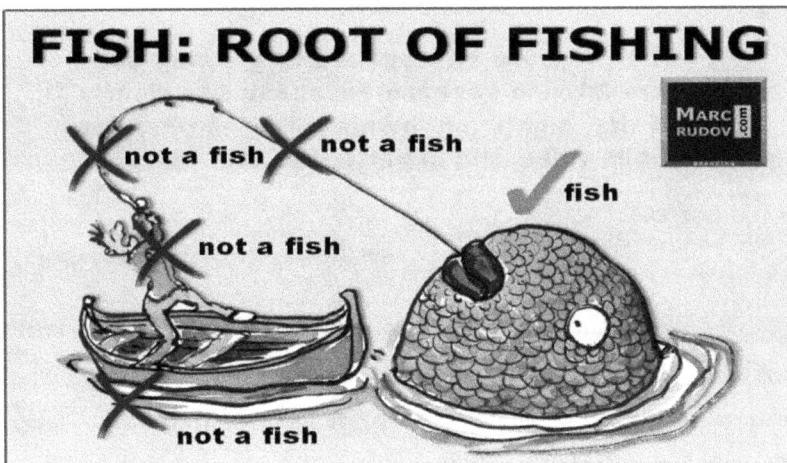

The line is not a fish. The pole is not a fish. The boat is not a fish. The fisherman is not a fish. *Only* the fish is a fish.

Regardless of country or language, this universal acceptance prevents misunderstandings. Seems simple, doesn't it?

Market also has only one meaning: *customers*, current and potential. Get that wrong and you'll jeopardize market*ing*, branding, which supersedes marketing—and, consequently, your company's destiny. Kind of important, right?

Yet, corporations, consultants, TV commentators, and business publications misuse market every day. I could fill an entire book with examples. Here's a recent one from *Fortune*.

FORTUNE

December 8, 2016

"The pressure on YouTube is growing even more intense because Facebook has clearly set its sights on owning the *market* for mobile video, and in particular live video."

Notice that I've italicized market—because there is no mobile-video market. It's called an *industry*. Market *never* refers to products, services, technologies, or industries—even though people mistakenly do so, everywhere, every day.

Market, the *demand* (customer) side of commerce, is people. Describe them by *their* characteristics, not yours.

Industry is the supply side. Market*place* is the nexus of the two. Confuse any of this, and you'll myopically focus on your products, instead of your customers. Such is the custom in Silicon Valley. This is *producting,* not marketing.

Market Research

Concomitant with our review of market is a revisit of market research, which means studying *people.*

A common misconception is that market research is about customers' and prospects' views and uses of products. And, why wouldn't that be the case, given how many people falsely believe a product is a market.

Market research comprises studying how *people* live and work, based on *their* characteristics and demographics, without the interjection of your company and its products or services or technologies.

By understanding the wishes, needs, and problems of *people* in all walks of life, in all occupations, clever enterprises then can devise the appropriate solutions.

Asking people to imagine products that will solve their problems or grant their wishes—*which too many in the business world believe is market research*—is futile. The job of conceiving products is *yours*, not your customers'.

As I stress numerous times and in numerous places throughout this book, understanding customers comes from *knowing* them, not reading their social-media posts. Create as many opportunities as possible to meet them, face-to-face.

Analyzing customers' perceptions, usage, praises, and criticisms of your products, once you conceive or build them, is called *product* research. Conducting product research, *without having done market research,* is a total waste of time.

So, never confuse market and product research, both of which your company must continuously undertake and perfect.

Varicose Arteries?

A useful way to reinforce the importance of using business terminology properly is to examine what happens in other fields.

Imagine practitioners in the legal and medical professions interchanging terms. Were a courtroom lawyer to utter opening *argument*, the judge would dismiss her, and colleagues would sneer at her. Arguments contain legalese, prohibited in statements. There are opening statements and *closing* arguments. Period.

Picture an MD discussing varicose *arteries*. She'd be ridiculed, disciplined, likely fired. Misusing and transposing medical terminology can harm, even kill, patients. Varicose *veins*, yes. Arteries? Never. Arteries and veins have different purposes and designs, as do markets and industries.

Think about these legal and medical examples the next time you blithely say "wireless market," which doesn't exist.

People say they buy food at the market, trade stocks on the market, put their houses on the market, and compete in the job market. These are **marketplaces**. Using the wrong terminology causes ambiguity, which begets failure.

Words Matter

MARKET

Any word that means *everything*, means *NOTHING*

MarcRudov.com

Bottom Line

To excel at marketing and branding, you must know the definition of market and ensure that your employees and advertising and PR contractors do likewise.

Imagine the skipper and crew of a yacht confusing starboard with port. Might there be chaos? I think so.

Establishing a profitable destiny depends on knowing and communicating the proper terminology.

CHAPTER THREE

Know Your Audience

Do you write and speak to everyone in the same way? Of course not. You must tailor both your message your and delivery—but not the message's essence—to the recipient's ability and desire to absorb and accept both.

Ah, but how do you ascertain an individual's ability and desire? Assume nothing. Study. Build a profile.

Accordingly, successful branding—the art and science of targeted messaging—hinges on knowing and connecting with your audience, your market. Reluctance or failure to do so will obscure your destiny and precipitate disaster.

Risk Profile

Nothing signifies the emotional component of buying, whether consumer or corporate, than customers' risk profiles.

Taking a risk is an *emotional* experience. Some people thrive on taking risks. Others run from risks, at all costs. Then, there are those who seek financial risks but avoid relationship risks and physical risks, and vice versa—and every other combination and permutation imaginable.

The objective is to know your audience, at every point in time, because the audience changes over time. As the audience changes, so does the degree of risk it will accept. That means your messaging must change accordingly.

Geoffrey Moore wrote a series of books, called *Crossing the Chasm*, to explain how distinct customer groups adopt new technologies over time, based on their risk profiles.

Moore's thesis is based on a previous book, *Diffusion of Innovations*, by Everett Rogers. In essence, the first customer group, comprised of *innovators*, will take the most risk in trying revolutionary products.

Laggards, at the right-most tail of adoption, are the most risk-averse. The early and late majority comprise the mainstream of customers. The biggest challenge is to cross the chasm between the early adopters and early majority. This is where most suppliers fail because they don't understand, and adjust to, the key differences in audience characteristics.

Coincidentally, risk behaviors of voters and customers are similar, and sharp politicians understand this.

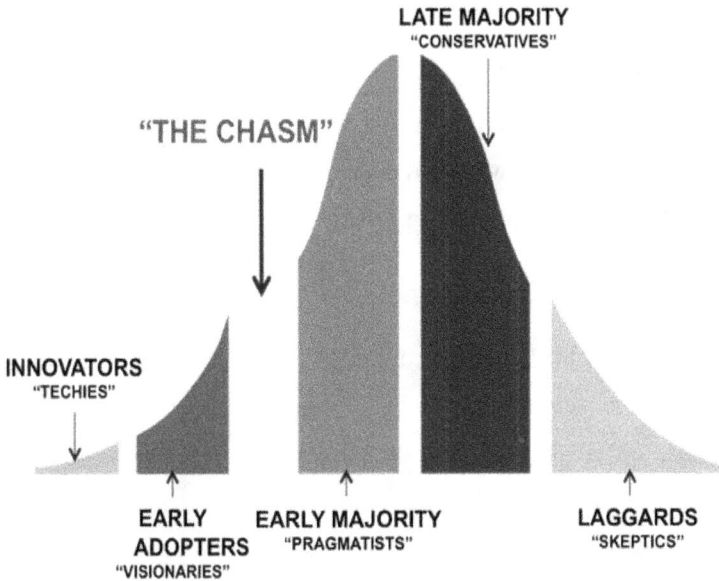

The 2016 Election

Most pollsters and pundits forecasting the outcome of 2016 presidential election, on the left and the right, dismissed and missed deep voter enthusiasm for a Trump victory.

Why?

They made the fundamental branding blunder: not knowing the audience.

Larry Sabato, highly esteemed pollster and director of the vaunted Center for Politics at the University of Virginia, incorrectly predicted a Clinton win. After the dust settled, he answered his critics: "We heard for months from many of you, saying that we were underestimating the size of a potential hidden Trump vote and his ability to win. We didn't believe it, and we were wrong."

If you don't know the audience, you don't know squat. Donald Trump knew the audience—the forgotten, neglected, frustrated, patriotic citizens—because he spent time with them at huge rallies, after they'd lined up for hours to see him.

This audience-ignorance phenomenon also has affected the advertising world, populated with progressive, coastal, elitist snobs and blindly dedicated to the infantile whimsies of Millennials.

On 11/21/16, the *Wall Street Journal*, in a telling piece, reported that ad execs are admitting they were out of touch with a huge slice of Trump's steadfast backers—rural, economically frustrated, elite-distrusting, anti-globalization voters—and are rethinking the way they collect data about consumers, recruit staff, and pitch products.

Right after the election, in which Donald Trump won 2,600 of America's 3,100 counties—and 83 percent of its geography—Harris Diamond, CEO of McCann Worldgroup, gathered his top execs to learn from the unexpected outcome. They concluded, for starters, that *too much advertising falsely assumes that all US consumers desire to be like coastal elites.*

Said Mr. Diamond:

"Every so often you have to reset what is the aspirational goal the public has with regard to the

products we sell. So many marketing programs are oriented toward metro elite imagery. Marketing needs to reflect less of New York and Los Angeles culture and more of Des Moines and Scranton."

It is one thing to be misinformed but quite another to be willfully ignorant, topped with contemptuous smugness. When Hillary Clinton derisively dumped Trump's followers into a "basket of deplorables," she committed this sin.

As McCann's Harris Diamond allowed, the advertising community—*which is highly paid to know the audience*—also sinned. And, that's why Trump's victory "surprised" them and why so much of their biased advertising fails.

There are three ways to address your audience: use time-tested, traditional nuggets, pique them with cleverness and boldness (my method), or infantilize them with political correctness—the modus operandi of America's everything's-offensive culture.

To know your audience, you must see and hear your audience. You also have to decide, objectively, if it's a stable and sustainable audience. Why? A fickle, infantilized crowd is neither stable nor sustainable and likely has little regard for your company.

Hint: Snowflakes who—because Donald Trump won the election, cry, skip classes, destroy property, and demand safe spaces where they can be comforted with coloring books, cocoa, bubbles, and puppies—fit this description.

Executives see and hear only what they choose to see and hear—based their social circles and biases—as McCann's Harris Diamond admitted above.

On this subject, actor Mark Wahlberg spoke to *Task & Purpose*, a magazine for veterans, about the irrelevance of political opinions from the Hollywood bubble:

> *"You know, it just goes to show you that people aren't listening to that anyway. They might buy your CD or watch your movie, but you don't put food on their table. You don't pay their bills. A lot of Hollywood is living in a bubble. They're pretty out of touch with the common person, the everyday guy out there providing for their family. Me, I'm very aware of the real world. I come from the real world, and I exist in the real world. And, although I can navigate Hollywood and I love the business and the opportunities it's afforded me, I also understand what it's like not to have all that."*

Knowing your audience is easy if your audience readily reveals itself. Sometimes, the audience is purposely silent—but that's no excuse for you to be uninformed. There are ways to grasp their thoughts, feelings, wishes, and grievances.

In the 2016 election, many Trump supporters, fearing harassment, ostracization, and injury, refused to admit their backing of the candidate to pollsters, journalists, friends, faculties, fellow students, work colleagues, and families. And, the demographics experts, like Larry Sabato above, completely missed this whole set of critical voter data.

But, the winner of the election, Donald Trump, missed nothing about these people. That and his ability and desire to talk to them—*in their language*—propelled him to victory.

Acknowledging that it had been ignoring the audience outside its bubble, Google, 10 days after the election, posted a job listing for a *manager of conservative outreach.* This was notable, considering its progressive bent.

Don't scoff. Google influences what the audience sees, believes, and does—or doesn't see, believe, and do.

WilkiLeaks exposed that Google, at the behest of its parent company's chairman, Eric Schmidt, helped guide Hillary Clinton's campaign. So did Timshel, a startup in which Schmidt is an investor. And, on election night, *Politico* posted a photo of Mr. Schmidt wearing a "staff" badge at Clinton's Javits Center "victory" party.

Cordcutters

The cable companies are guilty of audience ignorance as well. Today, we read and hear about cordcutters: those unsubscribing in droves from their cable-TV carriers. But, the reason most often given for this exodus is new technology.

Why would anyone waste money on cable, when he can watch a movie on a five-inch screen, wherever he happens to be located? Why indeed.

Does this make sense? No, it doesn't. It's bullshit.

The reason cordcutting is in vogue is simple: the cable companies arrogantly took their customers for granted and treated them badly. Their pent-up resentment became a trust problem for the carriers. Where there's no trust, there's no brand. Where there's no brand, there's no trust—and loyalty.

Because customers now have options, even suboptimal ones, they're exercising those options.

There's no substitute for watching a great movie on a widescreen TV, with a superior sound system to support it. But, many movie-watchers—especially Millennials, who can't or don't want to afford cable—are substituting anyway.

Had the carriers always connected with and respected their subscribers, and offered them bundle-rate options and multidevice viewing, said subscribers would have remained loyal and kept their cords and subscriptions intact.

Today, the carriers are falling all over themselves to stop the exodus—something they could have prevented easily and cheaply *with the right attitude and behavior.*

Trusting Nike

Contrast the trustless cordcutters with Nike's early running-enthusiast customers.

Nike's founder, Phil Knight, wrote a new book about his company's amazing history: *Shoe Dog*. In a compelling radio interview about his book with Fox News Channel's Brian Kilmeade, in May 2016, Knight shared the role that trust played in propelling Nike's growth.

First, Knight explained that his company wasn't just making sales. It was selling something that could help people perform better, to run longer and better. This message (brand) resonated with the running community.

He knew and connected with his audience.

Nike had the reputation in the running community of continuously improving its products. The fledgling company had a strong brand: Runners trusted Nike.

Nike, formerly known as Blue Ribbon, appeared at a sneaker tradeshow. It featured some shoes with ineffective innovations. Yet, people bought them anyway. Nike was the hit of the show.

Jeff Johnson, a Nike cofounder, couldn't believe it. He asked a group of customers why they would buy these shoes, despite their deficiencies. One attendee shot back: "We've been doing business with you for years. We know that you guys tell the truth. Everyone else BS's. You guys always shoot straight. So, if you say this new shoe is worth a shot, we believe."

Wells Fargo, the San Francisco-based bank, lost a boatload of trust for defrauding two million customers—it created fake accounts in their names, without their consents, to reach sales quotas. When caught, the bank fired 5,300 order-following employees, a total charade. It also "apologized" for the misdeeds, thinking the matter closed. Wrong. It incurred a $185 million fine, including a $100 million penalty from the Consumer Financial Protection Bureau, and canned the CEO. States, such as California and Ohio, suspended their business dealings with the bank. To win back that lost trust, Wells Fargo is futilely projecting a wholesome image via TV spots featuring its 19th-century horse-drawn stagecoach. Wells Fargo is mistakenly masking the issue with an obsolete image that won't resonate with a modern audience. It'll fail.

Contrast the destiny-killing actions of Wells Fargo and the cable carriers with the trust-building ones of Nike.

Bottom Line

No brand, no trust. No trust, no brand.

Knowing, respecting, and resonating with your target audience is at the heart of branding. Again, this axiom applies regardless of your company's industry, size, age, stage, and geography. Basic human behavior transcends all parameters. Emulate Nike, not Wells Fargo and the cable companies.

CHAPTER FOUR

Know Your Terrain

Choosing a destiny and creating a brand go hand-in-hand. But, without knowing the terrain your company must cross to near that destiny, plotting a course is futile.

What oceans, rivers, swamps, mountains, canyons, deserts, glaciers, competitors, and bandits stand in your way?

In commerce, your terrain includes these physical barriers—as well as taxes, regulations, economic conditions, business-friendliness (*Chief Executive* magazine: California is the worst state for business in USA), access to affordable capital, social instability, population wealth, and culture.

In February 2015, RadioShack, the iconic electronics retailer, filed for bankruptcy protection. It closed 1,700 stores and sold the remaining 2,400 stores to wireless carrier Sprint and Standard General, Radio Shack's leading lender.

Why did Sprint, which is struggling for survival, want to buy physical stores?

Perhaps you question the logic of Sprint's move. The so-called "experts" predicted that the Internet would obliterate bricks-and-mortar retailing. But, Xfinity (Comcast) and AT&T

also operate retail establishments, as does Apple. In fact, Apple brought in Angela Ahrendts, former CEO of Burberry, to run its stores. Must be important to Apple's brand.

Amazon.com, according to *Forbes*, is planning to greet more of its customers in physical stores. There will be Amazon book stores, Amazon food stores, Amazon pop-up stores, and maybe even Amazon fashion stores.

Physical stores offer *advantages* over online shopping. As you will learn in subsequent chapters, relying solely on the Internet for branding, selling, and research is foolish.

Without being on the ground, physically, a company loses human contact and terrain expertise.

Newsflash: Without face-to-face contact, you don't know what customers *really* think and feel, and what your competitors are doing—and you cannot succeed in branding.

CIA Parallels

There are parallels in America's Central Intelligence Agency, the CIA. Have you ever wondered why the USA is constantly surprised by terrorist events around the world? The reason: *lack of human intelligence on the ground.*

From the Cold War's demise in 1991 until the 9/11 attacks, the CIA lost funding, prestige—and its huge network of embedded spies. It relied instead on foreign intelligence agencies and technology, a huge blunder.

Brian Fairchild, a former CIA case officer, asserted: "Without actual people on the ground to gain 'actionable intelligence' on terror plots or terror-cell networks like the Islamic State and Al Qaeda, the US is essentially flying blind."

Economy & Competition

In 2008, more businesses died than formed for the first time in recorded history—because of taxes, regulations, a growing anti-business climate, and a decreasing willingness of would-be entrepreneurs to take risks. Since 2009, GDP growth and, naturally, confidence in business conditions have been anemic. Be aware of these trends.

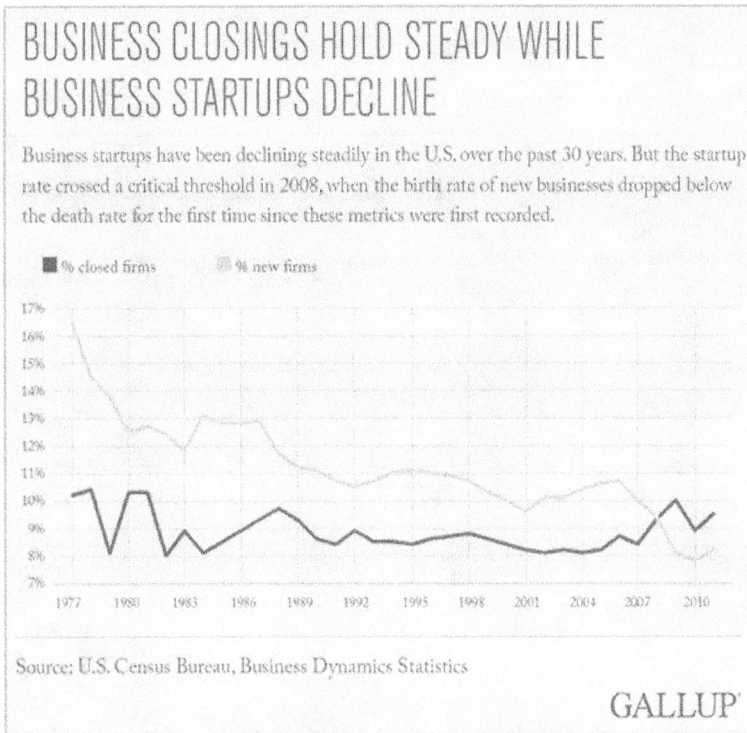

BUSINESS CLOSINGS HOLD STEADY WHILE BUSINESS STARTUPS DECLINE

Business startups have been declining steadily in the U.S. over the past 30 years. But the startup rate crossed a critical threshold in 2008, when the birth rate of new businesses dropped below the death rate for the first time since these metrics were first recorded.

■ % closed firms   % new firms

Source: U.S. Census Bureau, Business Dynamics Statistics

GALLUP

According to the National Federation of Independent Business, though, because of Trump's election, confidence is soaring at a level not seen since 1980, when Reagan became president. Can your brand leverage this sudden change?

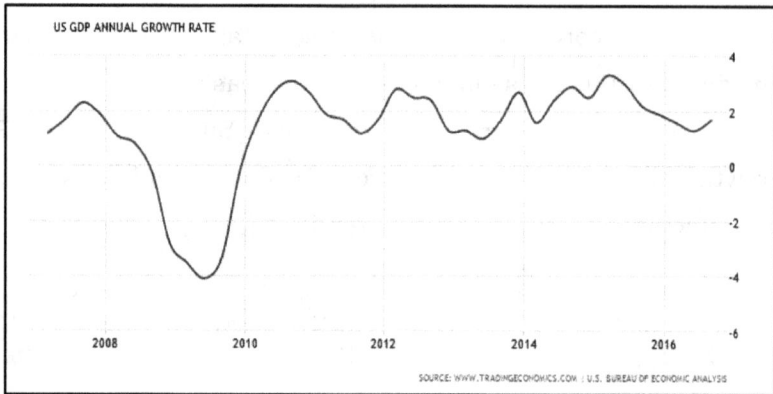

US GDP ANNUAL GROWTH RATE

SOURCE: WWW.TRADINGECONOMICS.COM : U.S. BUREAU OF ECONOMIC ANALYSIS

Brimming With Confidence
Small firms buy in to Trump's economic plans

■ Small-Business Optimism

Biggest monthly gain since July 1980

105.8

Index

■ Business Conditions Expectations ■ Sales Expectations

Highest since March 2002

50.0
31.0

Source: National Federation of Independent Business

Bloomberg

Many CEOs have told me that they're too busy for branding, that it's not a priority, that the economy prevents them from taking action now. All these excuses are nonsense.

When does branding matter? This is akin to asking when breathing matters. Answer: ***always***. Alas, what matters and what actually happens are too often unrelated.

As we see in the graphic below, good economies spur more competition, begetting more white noise, making it harder for each competitor to stand out—and making it more difficult for customers to choose one of them, even though the propensity to purchase is high. Because competitors tend to resemble and copy each other, their products and services become indistinguishable commodities.

Branding Matters: *Always*

Number of Competitors

		Lo	Hi
	Good	FLOOD OF NEW COMPETITORS	WHITE NOISE
State of Economy			
	Bad	STAGNATION & PRICE WARS	CONSOLIDATION & PRICE WARS

© 2017 MarcRudov.com

In good economies, when business and customer confidence is high, you'll see a flood of new competitors. How can you differentiate your company? Strong brand.

In bad economies, when the propensity to purchase is lower, competitors face stagnation and price wars, and many firms exit their industries or combine with their competitors.

Consolidation in the legal field is an excellent example: clients have the power to play one lookalike firm off the other lookalike firm for reduced fees. Winners have strong brands.

If you're a CEO who deems branding a postponable, low-priority activity, or an optional luxury, *now* is the time to change your position.

Accordingly, if you're a board member of a company whose CEO elects to postpone, downplay, or ignore branding, *now* is the time to force a reverse of this policy.

The terrain is unforgiving. Don't ignore it. Your destiny and bottom lines are at stake.

Branding, like breathing, matters always—but only if you want to beat your competitors, retain your customers, grow your business, and increase your profitability.

Astroturfing

Increasingly relying on social media to assess your terrain and reach your customers, therefore, is a faulty strategy. Like the CIA, you need feet on the ground.

Not only are social media filled with white noise and fake traffic, they're fixed and often biased. Think fake news.

Sharyl Attkisson, former CBS reporter, explained to a TED audience at the University of Nevada, in February 2015, how *astroturfing*—or fake grassroots movements funded by political, corporate, or other special interests—very effectively manipulates and distorts media messages. Said she:

> *What is astroturf? It's a perversion of grassroots, as in fake grassroots. Astroturf is when political, corporate, or other special interests disguise themselves and publish blogs, start Facebook and Twitter accounts, publish ads, letters to the editor, or simply post comments online—to try to fool you into thinking an independent, or grassroots, movement is speaking. The whole point of astroturf is to try to give the impression there's widespread support for or against an agenda, when there's not. Astroturf seeks to manipulate you into changing your opinion, by making you feel as if you're an outlier, when you're not.*

> *One example is the Washington Redskins name. Without taking a position on the controversy, if you simply were looking at news-media coverage of the course of the past year, or looking at social media, you'd probably have to conclude that most Americans find that name offensive and think it ought to be changed. But, what if I told you 71% of Americans say the name should not be changed. That's more than two-thirds.*

> *Astroturfers seek to controversialize those who disagree*
> *with them. They attack news organizations that publish*
> *stories they don't like, whistleblowers who tell the truth,*
> *politicians who dare to ask the tough questions, and*
> *journalists who have the audacity to report on all of it.*

Bottom Line

Know your terrain and the economic and competitive factors affecting it. Per the US Labor Department's Bureau of Labor Statistics: 95,102,000 Americans (62.7 percent)—a new record—were not in the labor force, in December 2016, 47,000 more than the month before; in one of every five American homes, nobody is employed.

Unemployed people can't buy your products.

Know what your customers *really* think and want, as well as how they express themselves, by intimately knowing, like a spy, what's happening on the ground, in the sea, and in the air. That means getting your company's "feet" out of the ivory tower, out of unreliable social media, into the real world.

There's no excuse for wrecking your ship through willful ignorance—by relying "on foreign intelligence and technology"—and then hitting an unanticipated iceberg.

CHAPTER FIVE

Conformity

The keys to knowing your audience are grasping their behaviors—rational and irrational, mature and immature, passive and aggressive, real and artificial—and choosing your reactions to those behaviors.

In 1951, Solomon Asch, a notable social psychologist, conducted an experiment at Swarthmore College, outside Philadelphia, to explore how social pressure from a majority group could convince an outnumbered person to conform. He used 50 male participants in 18 trials (12 rigged, six normal).

Asch put seven "insiders" and one innocent in a room together to compare the length of a line on one card with three on the other, where one of the three was identical in length.

The "insiders" *purposely* chose the wrong lines. About 75 percent of the innocents agreed *at least once* with those lies; 25 percent of them never did. In the six times the groups were composed of all innocents, with no peer pressure, only one percent of them gave the wrong answer.

Subsequently, most of the innocents admitted that, despite not believing their acquiescent answers, they betrayed themselves *for fear of ridicule*. A few confessed to self-duping: really believing the majority's wrong answers.

Minorities conform for one of three reasons: 1) desire to fit in; 2) belief that majorities are smarter; 3) fear of ridicule or reprisal. We see this in astroturfing and elsewhere.

Examples of conformity in the real world:

April 2014: The mobocracy of Mozilla, maker of the Firefox browser, forced its cofounder and CEO, Brendan Eich, to resign—*for having the "wrong" belief.* In 2008, Eich had supported California's Proposition 8, a ballot initiative designed to preserve traditional marriage. To help force that resignation, online-dating purveyor OK Cupid shamed its Firefox users into using other browsers for accessing the site.

June 2015: The University of California at Berkeley announced bans on common expressions, such as *America is the land of opportunity* and *the most-qualified person should get the job.* This is a major university banning speech. Let that sink in.

March 2016: Seventeen US attorneys general, led by New York's Eric Schneiderman, threatened legal action and huge fines against anyone denying man-made climate change, an unproven theory.

May 2016: A new law decrees that New York City businesses face fines up to $250,000 if they don't use gender-correct pronouns like "ze" and "hir" to refer to transgender employees and customers.

September 2016: Gabriel Moshenska, senior lecturer in archeology at University College of London (UCL), granted his students permission to skip lectures if *scary skulls of dead people or traumatizing accounts of their deaths* might "trigger" them. Aren't bones and skulls central to archeology?

What's happening? We've seen a rise in tyranny and the willingness to abide it, groups replacing individuals, and the widespread infantilization of Western societies People have become fragile snowflakes, easily and perpetually offended.

Hans von Spakovsky, a First Amendment and civil-rights authority, put this nonsense in historical perspective:

"Beginning in 1478, the Spanish Inquisition systematically silenced any citizen who held views that did not align with the king's. Using the powerful arm of the government, the grand inquisitor, Tomas de Torquemada, and his henchmen sought out all those who held religious, scientific, or moral views that conflicted with the monarch's, punishing the "heretics" with jail sentences, property confiscation, fines, and, in severe cases, torture and execution.

"One of the lasting results of the Spanish Inquisition was a stifling of speech, thought, and scientific debate throughout Spain. By treating one set of scientific views

as absolute, infallible, and above critique, Spain silenced many brilliant individuals and stopped the development of new ideas and technological innovations. Spain became a scientific backwater."

Mr. Von Spakovsky has described the acorn of political correctness (PC), a paradigm of conformity under which a small group of zealots or rulers dictates, or tries to dictate, societal attitudes, behaviors, and speech to the rest of us.

Under the tyrannical rubric of "social justice," PC controls what citizens can or cannot think, believe, feel, say, write, do, earn, and own—despite the rights guaranteed to them by, in America's case, the US Constitution. We don't live in 1478; it's now 2017. Yet, the examples above illustrate the shocking parallels to the oppressive Spanish Inquisition.

Groupfeel

Despite the freedom to be leaders, most people are followers, conformists: they crave to blend in, to be accepted. They fear that holding and expressing opinions differing from the "consensuses" of social, business, professional, academic, athletic, governmental, political, and religious organizations will engender discord, even rejection.

Fear of ostracization and isolation, for many people, outweighs any desires to excel, to outperform, to be unique, or to shine a light on the truth. Feelings trump facts.

Grasping this reality is critical to successful branding: it affects the behaviors of your customers, investors, and employees—who too often will do what's generally *perceived* as popular, "virtuous," and safe, not what's right or logical.

Take the focus group. It's a market-research method, typically conducted face-to-face in a conference room with 10 or so potential or actual consumers or voters. Corporations, lawyers, and politicians hire focus-group facilitators to discern attitudes about products, people, ideas, and trends.

A major drawback of the focus group is a behavior known as groupthink: one strong personality will influence the opinions of the anodyne participants, resulting in a false group opinion. Such is the antithesis of *thinking* and a factor of political correctness.

Newsflash: groups don't think; they *feel*. Groupthink is a misnomer, an oxymoron. Instead, collective, follower-based, emotion-driven behavior is *groupfeel*.

Mark V. Cannice, department chairman and professor of entrepreneurship and innovation at the University of San Francisco School of Management, once made this observation about venture capitalists (VCs), people who invest in startup companies: "When they're feeling good, they invest more."

Feeling good? And I'll bet you thought VC investing is purely about spreadsheets, ROI, team competence, scalability, and cool products. Not necessarily so.

You can't eliminate groupfeel—it drives a lot of human behavior—but, you *must* fathom it and decide how much you'll accept from your target customer audience. More important, you must diligently fight it *inside your company*, as it destroys critical thinking.

When trying to get customers, investors, and reporters jazzed about your product and company, as Steve Jobs masterfully did, groupfeel can work to your advantage—*if the underlying emotions are healthy, mature, and rational.*

Conversely, heed the perils of groupfeel rooted in unhealthy, immature, and irrational emotions—because you can't build a sustainable business around customers such as UCL's archeology students afraid of skulls (mentioned above) or Oxford's law students allowed to skip "distressing" lectures on cases involving violence and death.

Overton Window

The Overton Window is the brainchild of Joseph P. Overton, a former VP of the Mackinac Center for Public Policy, a Midland, Michigan-based think tank. It illustrates the range of policy ideas the public will accept at a given snapshot of time, fluctuating between more freedom and more tyranny.

The reading in the sliding Overton "window" is always predicated on the perceived majority opinion—the conformity quotient—of the moment.

Politicians, for the most part, go along to get along and rarely solve any real problems. To get or stay elected, they usually write or sponsor laws and make speeches they believe will not render them too extreme, in either direction.

In 2010, nothing could and did stop Obamacare. It was popular in theory, despite its government overreach. Now that people are seeing, in some cases, 100-plus-percent rate increases, unreachable deductibles, and inadequate medical-procedure coverage, not to mention the devastation to small businesses, public opinion has shifted to *more freedom*. Now, they feel safely in the majority, demanding that Obamacare be repealed and replaced.

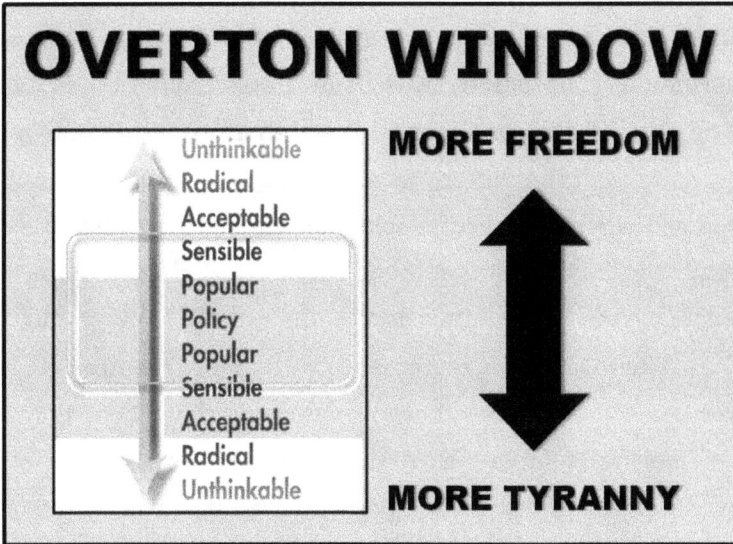

OVERTON WINDOW

Unthinkable
Radical
Acceptable
Sensible
Popular
Policy
Popular
Sensible
Acceptable
Radical
Unthinkable

MORE FREEDOM

MORE TYRANNY

Spiral of Silence

Another twist on the construct of conformity, as we've been discussing, is the Spiral of Silence (SOS) theory. Based on the *fear of isolation*, German political scientist Elisabeth

Noelle-Neumann proposed SOS in 1974. It explains why some people remain silent while others are more publicly vocal.

For example, many Trump supporters were afraid to expose themselves publicly, believing they were holding the minority viewpoint and would experience retribution.

Another example is the fear of publicly railing against man-made climate change, an unproven theory. In March 2014, Virgin Group chairman, Sir Richard Branson, exhorted businesses to "stand up" to climate-change deniers, who should "get out of our way." Apparently, Branson also was "enormously impressed" with Tim Cook, Apple's CEO, for telling climate-change skeptics to sell their Apple shares.

Such intimidation tactics from powerful, influential elites will silence a lot of people, convincing them that they're in the minority, pushing them further down the "spiral" of silence, where, eventually, they'll fade into the background.

The SOS works incrementally, as more members of the perceived minority see others remaining quiet. Then, they, in turn, fearing isolation, shut up. One is more likely to slide down the SOS if his stance doesn't *conform* to the *perceived* majority opinion—which emanates from social circles, social media, schools, workplaces, TV, movies, and news media.

On election night, because of SOS, the majority of pundits, pollsters, and media commentators had predicted a Clinton victory. *Newsweek* had printed, *in advance*, 125,000 copies with Madam President and Hillary's picture on the cover. Why? It was the "correct" opinion—and it was wrong.

In April 2015, Clorox created a bleach bottle from emojis, coincidentally on the day that Apple had released some brown-skinned emojis. The infantilized mob whined on social media that Clorox *had no right to be white* on such a momentous day. Instead of telling these snowflakes to piss off, Clorox's CEO caved and apologized for "offending" them.

BRANDING & FEAR DON'T MIX

MarcRudov.com

Newsflash: Branding and fear don't mix. Repeat this maxim daily: *If I can't take a stand, we don't have a brand.*

To wit: Ivanka Trump, eldest daughter of Donald Trump, designs and sells shoes for the working woman. She sells said shoes through a number of channel partners, one of which is Nordstrom. A bunch of women began to harass this retailer, in November 2016, to drop Ivanka's shoes—because they hate her father. Here's how co-president Pete Nordstrom responded to the mobocracy:

> *"We've heard from customers, including some who are long-time loyal customers, threatening a boycott of Nordstrom if we continue to carry the line. Similarly, we've heard from customers who say they will boycott Nordstrom if we stop carrying the brand. This is a sharply divisive subject. No matter what we do, we are going to end up disappointing some of our customers. Every single brand we offer is evaluated on their results—if people don't buy it, we won't sell it. And, since the Ivanka Trump brand has grown to be a sizable and successful business, it's not worth jettisoning, even if some of its customers feel passionately that it should. We strive to be agnostic about politics and to treat all our customers with respect."*

Consequently, the hysteria dissipated. **That**—not the Clorox way—is how a CEO must respond to the hysterical, tyrannical mobocracy, if it likewise attacks your business. Again, ***if you can't take a stand, you don't have a brand.***

Virtue Signaling

James Bartholomew claims he coined *virtue-signaling* in an April 18, 2015, article he wrote for the London-based *Spectator*. He defines it as "the way in which many people say or write things to indicate that they are virtuous. Sometimes it is quite subtle. By saying that they hate the *Daily Mail* or Ukip, they are really telling you that they are admirably non-racist, left-wing, or open-minded. One of the crucial aspects of virtue-signaling is that *it does not require actually doing anything virtuous.* It does not involve delivering lunches to elderly neighbors or staying together with a spouse for the sake of the children. It takes no effort or sacrifice at all."

In April 2014, Boko Haram, a radical Islamic extremist group, kidnapped 276 Nigerian girls. How did virtue-signalers respond? By hiring mercenaries? No. They tearfully tweeted the #BringBackOurGirls hashtag. Despite feeling virtuous and superior, while sacrificing zilch, they achieved nothing.

A spot-on episode of *South Park* called "Smug Alert!" cleverly epitomized virtue-signaling. The town's residents vied for virtue by driving hybrid cars *and denigrating those who didn't,* smelling their own farts, and smugly squinting.

In December 2016, Microsoft posted a "holiday" video on YouTube. This spot featured sympathetic images and anecdotes for Black Lives Matter, Syrian refugees, transgender activism, and more general LGBT issues.

Said Microsoft: "Our message focuses on the spirit of the holidays, people coming together, and celebrating what is good and right with the world—what unites us, instead of what divides us."

Lest you forget, Black Lives Matter advocates the killing of police officers. Syrian refugees have been raping women all over Europe. Celebrating what is good and right with the world?

Why would Microsoft post such a video during the Christmas holiday, offending traditionalists? Virtue-signaling. Microsoft has been enjoying a resurgence of success and stock-price appreciation, from Windows 10 and the Surface Pro computer.

What better way to appear "virtuous" (because success is deplorable), to divert attention from yucky capitalism, than to promote a politically correct, anti-capitalism message that makes its creators feel good about themselves.

Technological Correctness

We've already examined political correctness—control by governments, universities, and employers of our speech, attitudes, and actions. But, there's another form of control and conformity: *technological correctness*, or TC.

With TC, people are forced to accept technologies and the concomitant jargon, regardless of their merits.

For many years, cloud computing, which I've already addressed, has been shoved down our throats. Now, there's IoT (Internet of Things), which allows your toaster to talk to your vacuum cleaner via the Internet. Stupid name (IoT) and dangerous technology: it allowed hackers to cause a massive denial-of-service (DoS) attack on October 21, 2016.

The DoS attack—executed by infecting baby monitors, home routers, cameras, and other Internet-connected devices with software that flooded them with traffic—affected users on Twitter, Netflix, Spotify, Airbnb, *The New York Times*, Reddit, and Etsy. Criticize IoT, though, and prepare for rejection.

Take driverless cars. In October 2015, Steve Wozniak, cofounder of Apple, revealed his agenda of conformity at the Gartner Group symposium in Australia: "In 20 years, no human drivers will be *allowed* except for the young kids at Disneyland." He also opined: "In the future, self-driving cars will avoid problems humans make."

No human drivers allowed? Who appointed him czar of cars and citizens—and why? Wozniak's assertion that self-driving cars *will avoid problems humans make* is both absurd and disingenuous. First, fallible humans write, debug, and update the cars' software. Second, car computers, like PCs and smartphones, are easily hackable. Third, the electronic components enabling the software will malfunction at some point—from heat, age, or manufacturing flaws.

Moreover, not only can these "computers on wheels" malfunction and be hacked, causing massive traffic accidents and deaths, they can be monitored to control the owners' whereabouts and uses of fuel. Who wants this?

The US Department of Transportation has proposed a standard for enabling cars and light trucks to connect to each other wirelessly, ostensibly *to prevent hundreds of thousands of crashes every year.* The technology, known as vehicle-to-vehicle communications, or V2V, is expected to speed up the *push* toward driverless vehicles.

Will this extra regulation stop the mounting accidents, traffic violations, and death? In June 2016, a Florida man died when his self-driving Tesla S crashed into a truck.

Some tech execs and venture capitalists in Seattle—led by Tom Alberg, cofounder of Madrona Venture Group and Amazon board member, and Craig Mundie, former Microsoft exec—want to *ban* human drivers from a 150-mile stretch of Interstate 5 in Washington, in favor of driverless cars, trucks, and buses. Apparently, technology inspires tyranny.

Eric Hoffer, author of *The True Believer*, explains this well: "The men who rush into undertakings of vast change usually feel they are in possession of some irresistible power."

Well, the aforementioned men are pushing driverless cars onto society—rushing into undertakings of vast change—in cahoots with the major car companies, Apple, and Google. And, their technologically correct—and, so far, unchallenged—swagger suggests they possess feelings of irresistible power.

Alas, as passive people conform to such dictates and willingly become reliant on technology, much of it needless, they lose brain cells and spines. According to the Annenberg Public Policy Center, only 36 percent of Americans can cite the three branches of their government [despite having an unprecedented amount of information at their fingertips].

Albert Einstein noted, "Information is not knowledge."

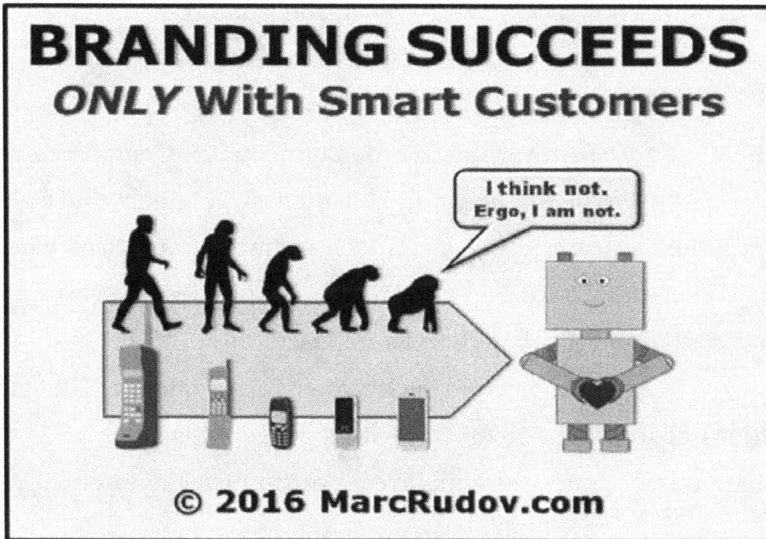

BRANDING SUCCEEDS
ONLY With Smart Customers

I think not.
Ergo, I am not.

© 2016 MarcRudov.com

Another blurry buzzword in massive use is *big data.* According to SAS Institute, a $3.2B software company in Cary, North Carolina, here's the definition:

> *Large volume of data, both structured and unstructured, that inundates a business on a day-to-day basis. But, it's not the amount of data that's important. It's what organizations do with the data that matters. Big data*

can be analyzed for insights that lead to better decisions and strategic business moves.

You'll notice that SAS's definition is gobbledygook, yet a Google search of this term yields 278-million listings. There are books, articles, and seminars trained on big data. What is medium data? What is small data? Nobody knows. Missing, as usual, from the term itself and its definition: *customer.* I hate to be a party-pooper, but, who is the customer? What's the problem you're solving? Doesn't matter. Conform or die.

A big driver of TC is Gartner Group, a $2B research and consulting firm in Stamford, Connecticut. Companies vie to occupy Gartner's Magic Quadrant (MQ)—which touts the "superior" suppliers in a given tech segment—and brag when they succeed. To inhabit the MQ, each supplier *must* use the Gartner jargon (I call it *Gargon*) imposed on it.

I can fill a book on technological correctness (TC), but we must move on. Remember it, though, when you see and hear yourself, and your employees, getting sucked into it.

Bottom Line

To succeed, you must assess the world inside (see Chapter Six) *and* outside your firm. Carefully choose your conformity credo, strategy, and tactics.

Surrendering to pervasive, omnidirectional pressures to conform will destroy your company's brand and its bottom line—and your executive authority.

CHAPTER SIX

Millennial Mania

I'm a Baby Boomer. When I entered the professional workforce, my generation was the largest cohort in America. Yet, the waters never parted for us. *We* were expected to be adults, to adapt to our employers' environments. *We did.*

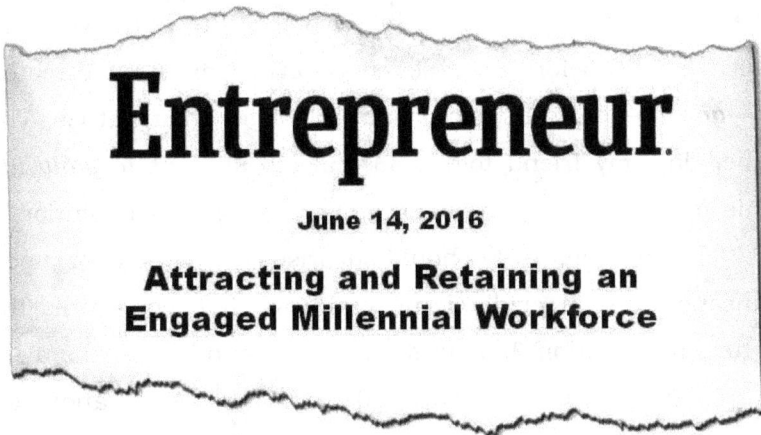

Entrepreneur.

June 14, 2016

Attracting and Retaining an Engaged Millennial Workforce

Today's largest cohort, Millennials, those of Generation Y, born between 1981 and 2000, are infantile. They've been constantly coddled and cosseted since birth, never forced to learn that frustration, failure, and criticism are part of life.

Companies are replacing doting parents and teachers, endlessly indulging these snowflakes, who grew up receiving participation trophies.

Read the business press. Articles abound about CEOs and HR execs maniacally *revering* Millennials, reorganizing their companies around them, and fighting their competitors to attract, retain, and please them. What could go wrong?

A friend of mine runs a program in a medical-trade school. Many of the students are already university-educated, hail from wealthy families, and are in their late-20s and early 30s. They're attending this school to get retrained in a field that actually offers jobs.

My friend tells me daily about the female students who line up, one at a time, to cry in her office. Why? They've never failed exams before or experienced criticism. They threaten to—*and do*—bring in their parents to fight their battles. The other day, my friend told a 33-year-old student *to grow up*. This student recoiled in horror, not grasping the admonition.

This immaturity should surprise nobody. It's not just a nuisance; it's an epidemic of weakness that jeopardizes the future of education, business, parenting, and life in general.

Dan Jones, past president of the Association for University and College Counseling Center Directors, agrees:

> *"Students haven't developed skills in how to soothe themselves, because their parents have solved all their problems and removed the obstacles. They don't seem to have as much grit as previous generations."*

Millennial Facts

The irony of Millennial Mania is startling, considering the unflattering facts about this coddled cohort. It is critical to understand these immature behaviors if you, the CEO, expect Millennials to be the basis of your company's bottom line.

Millennials are fragile snowflakes who demand and get safespaces (with coloring books, Play-Doh, and videos of frolicking puppies) to help them recover from traumas, such as Trump's victory. They demand and get trigger warnings—in their textbooks and novels, and on campus signs—to protect them from "offensive" speech and ideas: *microagressions*.

Psychiatrist and Harvard University professor Chester Pierce coined "microaggression" in 1970 to characterize the insults he regularly witnessed whites inflicting on blacks.

Eventually, microaggression would mean *any* smear (who decides?) of *any* socially demeaned group (who decides?), with the perpetrator able to offend casually or unknowingly. Now, nearly every form of expression is deemed offensive.

Example #1: A white student asks an Asian student to help him with his math homework. By doing so, the white student "injures" the Asian student. How? By assuming he fits the stereotype of all Asians excelling in math. Seriously.

Example #2: A white student wears a sombrero to and sings mariachi music at a college-campus Halloween party. He's guilty of "cultural appropriation," insulting all Mexicans, and has, therefore, committed a microaggression. Oops.

Surprising Millennial Developments & Facts

Educational Testing Service (ETS), provider of SAT tests: American Millennials, compared with their peers in 23 other nations, are among the weakest in the skills employers want most: literacy (including ability to follow simple instructions), practical math, and problem-solving in technology-rich environments.

Emory University president Jim Wagner had to soothe snowflakes aggrieved by "Trump 2016" chalk messages on campus sidewalks: They voiced *genuine concern and pain in the face of this perceived intimidation.*

Administrators at Yale, Cornell, Syracuse, Vassar, and Oberlin ripped up copies of the Constitution, handed out off-campus, after an impostor student described the document as "triggering" and "oppressive."

According to the *New York Times*, almost 40 percent of Millennials said cereal is an inconvenient breakfast choice because they have to clean up after eating it.

PayScale surveyed 76,000 employers in 2016 about college graduates: 60 percent said grads lack critical-thinking skills; 56 percent said they lack attention to detail; 44 percent said grads are poor writers; and 39 percent said they're weak at public speaking.

UCLA law students were *traumatized*, in 2014, over a constitutional-law exam question about the shooting in Ferguson, Missouri. *The professor later apologized.*

Comedians Jerry Seinfeld and Chris Rock no longer perform at universities because of political correctness: the fragile students are offended by every joke.

Boston College professor Peter Gray: *"America's college students are delicate, immature wusses who become traumatized, get the vapors, and seek professional counseling any time they face adversity or—God forbid—earn a grade lower than a 'B.'"*

Millennials are the least-entrepreneurial generation in recent history. The share of under-30 business owners has fallen by 65 percent since the 1980s, according to a *Wall Street Journal* analysis of Federal Reserve data.

Responding to "heartfelt notes" of students "in shock" over Trump's election victory, a Yale professor made that day's exam optional.

Cal State University, Los Angeles, established "healing" spaces for students to cope with the pain caused by a political speech *delivered three months earlier.*

Millennials, on average, hold $37K in college debt. Compared to Boomers at the same stage of life, they're worth half as much and earn 80 percent as much, despite being "better educated."

45% of college-educated Millennials work at jobs not requiring college degrees.

Trulia: About 40% of Millennials were living with their parents in 2015, the largest percentage since 1940.

Adulting

A recently created term describes the instructions that help clueless snowflakes grow up in our infantilized society: *adulting*. Seriously. There are books on this subject and a business called The Adulting School in Portland, Maine.

No, adulting isn't meant for unruly teenagers, as one might expect. It's for Millennials (up to age 34), who don't know how to cook, clean, do laundry, pay bills, make doctors' appointments (and show up on time), and live independently of their parents—*and don't realize that they're supposed to.*

This is what happens when children have helicopter parents, are spared from disappointments and failures, get participation trophies, and never hear the word *no.*

In a politically correct world, where people on one side have a *fear of offending*, what I call FOO, and babies on the other who find everything offensive, branding can't work.

Branding requires creativity, boldness, and risk. It means challenging and often piquing the audience. None of this is possible when dealing with the interminably immature.

How do you break this logjam of fear? If both sides continue living trepidatiously, you cannot.

When petulant students at Ohio State staged a sit-in at the office door of Michael Drake, the university's president, unlike his feeble colleagues around America, he threatened jail and expulsion. The snowflakes, unaccustomed to criticism and challenge, melted and obeyed his order. Problem solved.

You, the CEO, should emulate Michael Drake. Instead of coddling fragile snowflakes—*whether they're customers or employees*—demand and accept only adult behavior from them. They'll respond accordingly. Really, they will.

In other words, become a FOO-fighter. FOO, the fear of offending, is a worldwide plague. Don't participate. There's no method of adulting better than a swift kick in the ass.

Sadly, because of FOO, perpetual victimhood is the new norm in our spineless culture, and so-called adults are devolving into Millennials. Maturity is becoming extinct.

To help New York City's municipal workforce deal with election-year "stress and vulnerabilities," induced by Donald Trump's victory, Mayor Bill de Blasio is offering them "free" (taxpayer-funded) counseling services and resources.

Dr. Keith Ablow, a prominent psychiatrist and author, reacted to Mayor de Blasio's infantilization nonsense:

> *"Taken literally (and we should), the mayor is telling citizens of New York City that they should indulge any potential weakness inside them that makes them believe they can't deal with the results of American democracy, when the results don't go their way—that they're easily injured, inherently weak, and don't have the personal fortitude to keep fighting for what they believe in."*

Bottom Line

Remember: a company with an infantile workforce is unsustainable; a company with an infantile customer base is unsustainable.

Helming an unsustainable company is a futile venture, which will degrade your brand, your destiny, and, thus, your bottom line. Either you fight your FOO or wallow in poo.

CHAPTER SEVEN

Know Your Company

Rebecca Homkes, teaching fellow at London Business School, and MIT Sloan School senior lecturer Don Sull wanted to learn how well companies execute their strategies. The duo asked more than 11,000 senior executives in 400 firms to name their top-three priorities. Only about one-third could do so and, given five tries, only about half could agree on one.

These results don't surprise me. I was lecturing a group of CEOs and asked: *Were you to query your employees, at all levels, about why your company exists and how it's unique, what would they say?* The reaction from the room: blank stares, crickets, and palpable awkwardness.

First, the CEOs couldn't have answered my question, either: their companies were brandless. Second, intracompany communication is universally poor—and CEOs don't realize it.

Translation: too many CEOs, *and their employees*, do not know their own companies. This is akin to paratroopers landing at night in a foreign country—with no idea why, no knowledge of the terrain, and no clue about what each should do next. This is when "self-management" and chaos begin.

I cannot reiterate my immutable axiom frequently enough: With no brand, a murky brand, or a horrible brand—whether extant by design or default—your destiny shall be endless random drifting or hitting an iceberg. Either way, your bottom line is imperiled.

Design or default? Yes. Some people work hard, with a touch of ignorance, arrogance, or defiance, to build a defective brand. Others achieve this ignoble outcome by doing nothing.

End Your Entroprise

Getting lost while driving, for goal-oriented people, is a maddening, time-wasting experience. We've all been there and hate it. Tempers flare. Opportunities vanish. Deals implode. Schedules crumble. Reputations teeter. Chaos abounds.

Maps and GPS services exist to help us avoid such chaos. But, navigation tools are useful only if they're accurate and properly employed.

Many a company, unfortunately, is driving while lost—either because the CEO's a good driver with a bad itinerary (destiny) or a poor driver, period, even with a good itinerary.

Regardless of why it's adrift, dealing with a lost enterprise, from the inside or the outside, is a maddening, time-wasting experience. It's pure chaos.

Newsflash: Absent a valid and crystal-clear destiny (brand)—*and the resolve, resources, and ability to pursue it*—chaos is around the corner for every enterprise.

Chaos, or entropy, in the enterprise is a success-killer: It angers and enervates those who buy from, invest in, write about, partner with, supply, and work at your company.

Entropy drives patrons to go elsewhere and employees to build fiefdoms, go rogue, sabotage, and battle each other in the dreaded internecine wars—all of which decimate your top and bottom lines. In other words, entropy is a brand-killer.

The entropy-inflicted enterprise is an **entroprise**, a term I coined and, you'll recall, introduced in Chapter One. In an entroprise, the left and right hands are unacquainted.

Entroprises make bad hiring decisions, resist firing incompetent employees, implement poor policies, are slothful, develop off-target or inferior products, and are impossible to fathom and distinguish from their competitors.

Are you a chief *entroprise* officer?

The acorn of the entroprise: the defective (nonexistent, nebulous, or horrible) brand. When employees get no direction or confusing or bad direction, they respond chaotically, in ways that *they* choose, ways that harm your business.

That said, sometimes the brand *is* crystal-clear, but the navigation system or the navigators betray it. Apple Maps, for example, has taken me and millions of others to incorrect locations and deadends, because of faulty algorithms or data.

Likewise, inexperienced marketing teams make false assumptions and use faulty logic—putting their companies' strong brands in jeopardy. This can happen when firms grow rapidly and hire new employees faster than execs can properly vet, train, and task them.

Example: Impulsively using ineffective social media as branding and selling megaphones, swallowing the false hype that these conduits have supplanted traditional megaphones.

Often, CEOs don't know about problems like this until they fester. That's why knowing your company is paramount.

Other times, the CEO injects false assumptions and faulty logic of his own into the mix.

On March 4, 2016, *Fortune's* Jennifer Reingold wrote a scathing piece about Zappos, the online shoe retailer owned by Amazon. Once considered a "Best Company to Work For," Zappos had fallen from grace. Why?

Tony Hsieh, the CEO, replaced traditional hierarchical management with self-management: a *holocracy.* Nonsense.

Newsflash: People can't manage themselves—*they just can't.* Perhaps you can guess what happened next.

After one year, almost one-third of Zappos's employees had bolted. Morale sank. And, those who remained responded negatively to *Fortune's* destiny-centric survey question: *Do you think management has "a clear view of where the organization is going and how to get there"?* Shocking!

Imagine any high-level sports team winning one game without an authoritative, order-spewing coach. You cannot. It is impossible. Evidently, Zappos imagined the undoable.

Don't create an entroprise—or allow one to develop or persist. Constantly monitor your company's level of entropy—its *cost of chaos,* its cost of being lost—then, nip it in the bud.

SWOT Analysis

A diligent CEO must verify that her company is moving toward its destiny. The balance sheet and income statement give a bottom-line snapshot but not much strategic insight.

For that, enterprises routinely assess their strengths, weaknesses, opportunities, and threats—all of which are *both external and internal.*

This essential exercise, known commonly as the SWOT analysis, must be conducted objectively and honestly—or is a total waste of time.

SWOT analysis is so fundamental that it's one of the first tools a business-school professor teaches to a new crop of MBA students.

SWOT-analysis practitioners present their findings and conclusions in a four-box matrix. It is a dynamic analysis: what happens in one box affects the other three.

Moreover, populating the SWOT matrix cannot and, therefore, must not be done in a vacuum.

Strengths and weaknesses based on what? Threats and opportunities based on what? Context is required. A reference is required. That context, that reference is *brand*.

In a top-down view of the diagram below, we see that the brand resides in a level *above* the S-W-O-T blocks—because the brand dictates what the blocks contain, how the blocks interact, and what the final analysis yields.

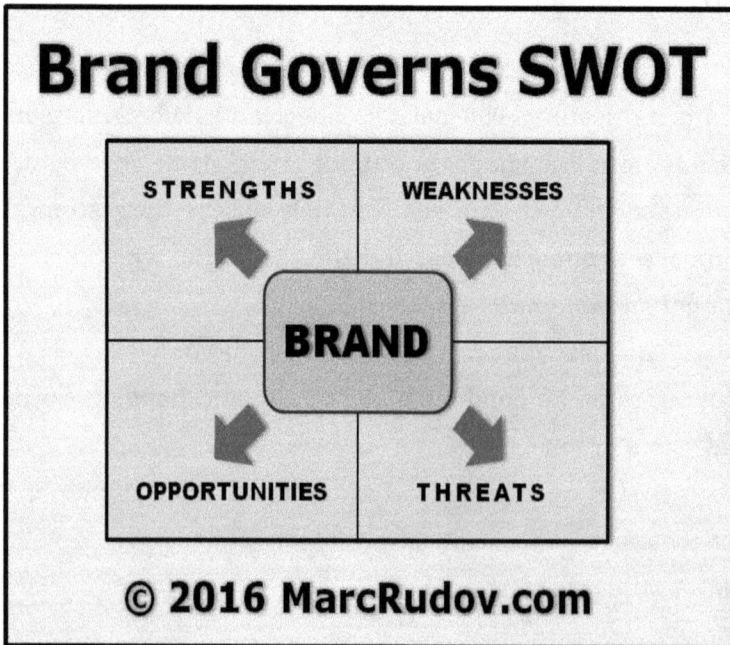

Brand Governs SWOT

STRENGTHS   WEAKNESSES

BRAND

OPPORTUNITIES   THREATS

© 2016 MarcRudov.com

Newsflash: Not knowing and incorporating your brand into the SWOT analysis renders it virtually worthless.

It's likely you've never considered this point until now and, henceforth, will make brand-centered SWOT mandatory.

A strong, unique brand will increase the number and kind of strengths and opportunities, and decrease the number and kind of weaknesses and threats. The converse is also true. That's why branding is the CEO's #1 priority.

Revisit, in Chapter One, the figure entitled "Brand Outranks You." Your company's brand *must* dictate the people you hire; products you design, build, and sell; and processes you implement—all of which have internal and external attributes, all of which affect your SWOT analysis.

Only if customers deem it so is your company's brand unique, compelling, memorable, repeatable, and commercially effective. When assessing it, they factor in your competitors; the economy; *their* needs and wants; and *their* experiences with, impressions of, and trust in your company.

Again, assembling a team to perform a SWOT analysis, sans brand, will yield little pertinent, actionable information and, thus, can't point your company—*and keep it pointed*—toward its destiny.

So, if your company's brand is in need of repair or creation, take care of it *before* initiating a SWOT analysis.

Finally, review your company's past SWOT analyses, those conducted *without* incorporating the brand. Be honest: Do they now make any sense?

Enterprise Personality

Many moons ago, right out of engineering school, I landed as a manufacturing engineer at the Eastman Kodak Company in Rochester, NY. After toiling awhile on a movie projector and an electronic flash for the short-lived instant camera, I began to contemplate my future. So, I ambled down to my least-favorite department, HR, where I expressed to the available puke my desire to pursue an MBA. I also requested confirmation that Kodak would pay for it.

He pointed to a portrait on the wall and asked me to identify the man in the frame. "Walter Fallon," I replied. "And do you know his title?" he continued. "I believe he's the CEO," I rejoined. "That's right. Walter Fallon is the CEO, and he's a chemist. He didn't need an MBA to succeed here, and neither do you. Now, you can go get an MBA, and we'll probably pay for it, but I counsel against it."

His attitude stunned me. I walked back to my desk, dejected, wondering what kind of company I had joined.

By blowing me off, the snarky HR rep had revealed Kodak's "personality." Every company has one, and it usually stems from the CEO. In an old company like Kodak, the personality is ingrained via a series of same-thinking CEOs.

I shelved my plans to get an MBA for a few years until after moving to Boston and working for another company.

Kodak filed for Chapter 11 bankruptcy in 2012. The prominent personality traits—*arrogance and insularity*—that effected this implosion were obvious when I worked there.

The figure below depicts *enterprise personality*. Every company has either an external (customer) bias or an internal (corporate) bias. Every company also either blindly *follows* trends (whatever Millennials do is fantastic) or *decodes* them (Millennials are broke, in debt, infantilized, and living with their parents; maybe we shouldn't bet our company on them).

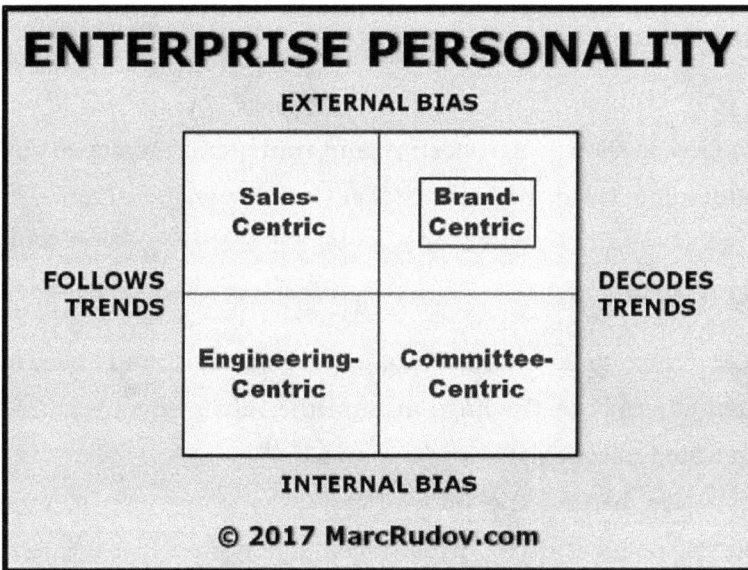

ENTERPRISE PERSONALITY

EXTERNAL BIAS

	Sales-Centric	Brand-Centric	
FOLLOWS TRENDS			**DECODES TRENDS**
	Engineering-Centric	Committee-Centric	

INTERNAL BIAS

© 2017 MarcRudov.com

A brand-centric company, like Disney, is the prototype for excellence: it has an external bias and decodes trends.

3M, an engineering-centric enterprise, is known as an adhesives company. Most of its product ideas begin in the lab. The company currently is struggling with stagnancy.

GoPro, cited in Chapter One, is sales-centric and, after soaring, is in decline. The Gap, also cited in Chapter One, is a committee-centric company: constrained, bland, and flailing.

There are two critical factors in enterprise personality: 1) knowing what it is; 2) aligning it with your core customers.

If you don't know your enterprise's personality or are in denial about it, wake up, ASAP. Decipher it. Analyze it.

Assuming you know said personality, is it optimally suitable for your target customers? If not, change it, ASAP—even if you, the CEO, find doing so uncomfortable.

Again, becoming a *brand-centric enterprise*—regardless of your industry, market, geography, age, or size—will help you choose the optimal destiny and route, and maximize your bottom line. Heed this advice. *Don't become another Kodak.*

HQ Mania

Next time you're sitting in yet another staff meeting, listen carefully to the lingo around the table. How much of it is devoted to *customers and their needs*?

I'm betting the bulk of it is about org charts, office politics, political correctness, incompetent employees, jargon, healthcare, beer blasts, products, and technologies.

Moreover, it's likely that the attendees' consensus will be to schedule *more meetings*—instead of resolving issues.

Congratulations: Your cozy company has *HQ mania*.

The hard-charging execs who found a company bear little resemblance to the soft employees who join it years later.

The founders are totally obsessed with finding *paying* customers to fund the rent, light, and payroll. They have no option but to know what customers think, feel, want, say, and do—no coincidence, *the ingredients of a brand.* Founders make personal sacrifices by working excessively long hours, and they often don't pay themselves at first.

Over time, success allows the firm to occupy fancier digs and hire new employees, typically focused on benefits and balanced lives—not on the firm's survival.

Gradually, the bias shifts from the outside world to the inside world. Use of jargon multiplies exponentially. Way-too-comfortable employees don't promptly, or ever, respond to phonecalls and emails, and they become snarky about their company's products and success.

Moreover, as the founders grow to be busy managers and ego-soothers, and wealthy, conspicuous consumers, they, too, start detaching from the details of activities and events occurring outside the HQ's walls. Yes, they admit this to me.

Here's why you, the CEO, should care: HQ mania kills brands. A defective brand, as we've discussed, points you to a suboptimal or dangerous destiny and hurts your bottom line.

As time evolves for the typical enterprise, the mirror of hubris gradually supplants its original window of opportunity.

Apathy replaces action. HQers nest in their cubicles. They see only *their* reflections—even in customers' faces—and become detached and, inevitably, insulated from the external world. Corporatespeak dominates all their conversations.

Result? They grow soft and uncompetitive. They know little about their customers and prospects—what they think, feel, want, say, and do—as evidenced by their blind zeal for impersonal, unsocial media. Although common, and too often tolerated, this is an unsustainable business model.

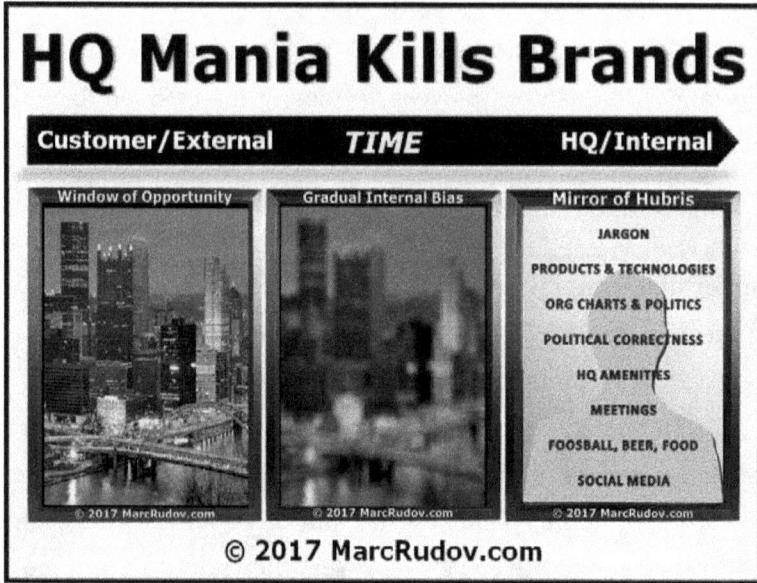

© 2017 MarcRudov.com

Apple is currently in danger of succumbing to HQ mania. Its ivory toroid, still under construction, is proof.

When companies become inwardly focused and biased, as depicted in the figure above, they unwittingly convert their windows of opportunity to mirrors of hubris—and cripple their branding machines.

Nothing makes a firm more internally biased than over-the-top office space; that is what Apple is erecting. Once they occupy this paradise, Apple employees, undoubtedly, will be too comfortable, pampered, and detached from the external world to brand successfully.

Scrutinize the megaphones of insular enterprises: homepages, brochures, PR, advertising, conferences, media interviews, speeches, and Twitter posts. Notice the degree to which they talk to and about themselves, and *build products to satisfy their egos, cultures, and legacies.*

Apple is building such a mirror of hubris, literally and figuratively, on 176 acres in Cupertino, CA. Scheduled to open in the second quarter of 2017, its doughnut-shaped future headquarters, sporting a one-mile circumference, will boast a 90,000-square-foot cafeteria and house 13,000 employees.

In December 2015, Jony Ive, chief design officer, and Tim Cook, CEO, gave a revealing tour of Apple's solar-powered "spaceship" to Charlie Rose, a correspondent for CBS's *60 Minutes.*

One couldn't help but be impressed with the new HQ's architecture and functionality, which Steve Jobs and Jony Ive conceived. But, as the tour progressed, I grew uneasy with its lavishness. For example, Ive designed oak chairs and desks that, at the touch of a button, can be lowered or raised.

My tipping point emerged when Ive began to gush about using the world's largest curved glass in the circular edifice—*and requiring a special-built machine to install it*—which has nothing to do with understanding and serving customers, and beating the competition.

I saw a huge complexity in this outrageous edifice: It's so self-serving. Apple's demise may be nigh.

Apple employees will feel transported and elevated while occupying their self-aggrandizing spaceship. They'll be arrogantly high-fiving themselves and each other—and, trust me, disparaging those not likewise privileged to inhabit it.

Think I'm exaggerating? Just wait.

Remember: The fancier your headquarters, the weaker your employees and company.

Success in branding requires external focus and bias—*and the ability to maintain that focus and bias.*

Corporate Risk

Passengers on the Titanic most certainly felt that their captain was running a tight ship. Everything around them likely seemed tidy and orderly.

Imagine the gleaming gears, shiny pistons, and well-trained men stoking the boilers in its state-of-the art engine room.

A "tight ship," as the Titanic tragedy revealed, is not necessarily pointed in the right direction, or moving at a judicious and sustainable speed, or run by a crew able to spot, avoid, and obliterate hazardous obstacles ahead.

The "unsinkable" Titanic fit this profile: eventually colliding with an iceberg, sinking, and killing 1503 passengers and crew.

As I analogized in this book's preface and beyond, corporations are ships. Many of them quickly and efficiently negotiate the wrong destinies—mostly because they haven't defined and articulated them.

Without a strong brand, a clear direction, where's your ship or truck or jet headed?

Many corporate captains, CEOs, equate product with purpose, forcing their enterprises to change direction and messaging frequently. IBM is a great example with cloud, big data, mobile, social, and Watson. Results: Its revenues have declined for 19 straight quarters, as of January 2017.

In 1983, Apple's board hired John Sculley away from Pepsi, where he was CEO, to helm the flailing computer company. He was out of his depth. He tinkered plenty in the engine room but never established a strong brand. So, no employees understood the rationale for any of Sculley's directives. Twenty-seven years later, in 2010, Sculley admitted that he had almost destroyed Apple.

By failing to create strong brands, instead focusing on their "engine rooms," CEOs burden their enterprises with substantial risks, rendering them vulnerable to destruction.

The discipline associated with minimizing corporate risk is called risk management. According to the International Organization for Standardization (ISO), risk is *the effect of uncertainty on objectives.*

Is there a bigger cause of uncertainty than having an unclear direction? No. Yet, those in the risk-management field don't speak about brands and branding. They should.

Examine the brand-risk polarity in the figure below. Brand and corporate risk are inversely related. This is logical: the more nebulous your direction, the more vulnerable your ship—and vice versa.

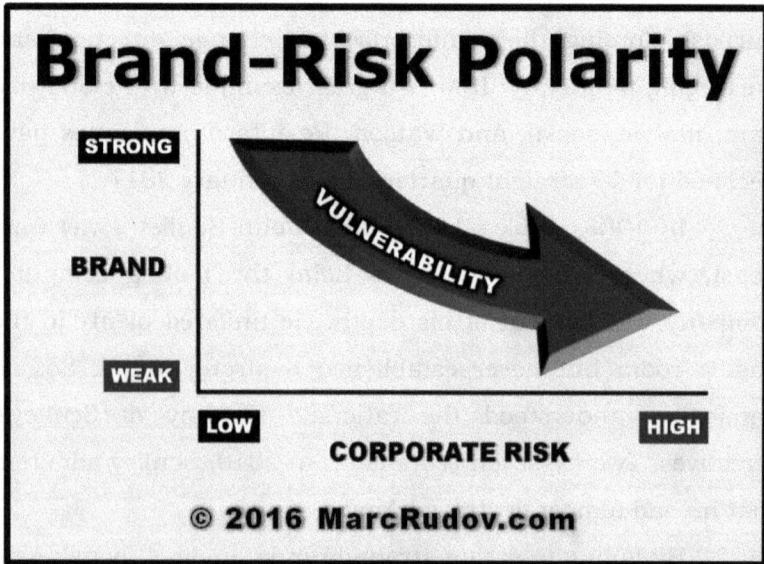

© 2016 MarcRudov.com

There are many kinds of risk: operational, financial, economic, human, political, geographical, etc. I can distill the long list into four easy-to-remember categories: *internal, external, tactical, and strategic.*

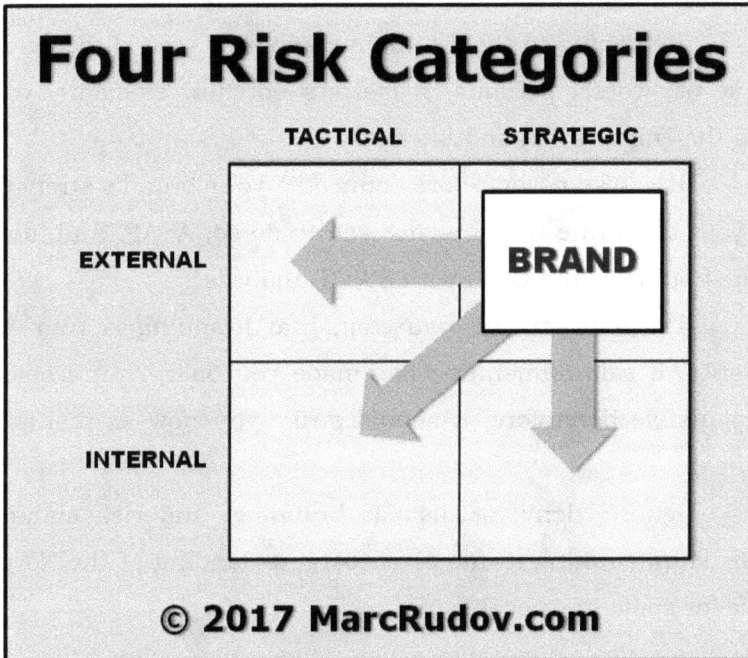

Four Risk Categories

TACTICAL   **STRATEGIC**

EXTERNAL   **BRAND**

INTERNAL

© **2017 MarcRudov.com**

External vs. internal is straightforward. Some risks, say financial, are hybrids. An action is tactical if it's short-term, reversible, and the CEO can easily and quickly cancel it.

The customer-derived brand is external and strategic: it requires a long-term commitment. Remember this next time you observe a company change its messaging with every product introduction.

But, despite being conceived from external forces, your brand affects internal activities, both tactical and strategic: products built, people hired, and processes implemented.

Also, based on the compounding effect of intertwining activities and their attached risks, the degree of overall corporate risk caused by a weak brand can be catastrophic.

Returning to the Titanic metaphor: If your direction is futile or, worse, perilous, it matters not how efficiently you run the engine room and kitchen.

If you've never before connected your brand's strength to your corporate risk, I advise you to do so, ASAP. And, now you should see the tie-in with SWOT analysis.

I've told you, ad nauseam, that branding is your #1 priority. If said admonition has made you balk, or it seemed implausible heretofore, it should strike you now as real and critical.

Ignore, deny, or dismiss branding, and risk sinking your ship, running it into an iceberg, or landing at the North Pole for some inexplicable reason.

Bottom Line

Know your company, its brand, its risks, its strengths and opportunities, and its personality. End your entroprise.

Destroy your company's fatal mirror of hubris, and restore its window of opportunity: Force your employees to leave their cozy desks to make *direct, personal customer contacts* (Hint: Twitter isn't direct, personal contact).

Your enterprise *must* be a lean, mean profit machine, a decoder—*not a follower*—of trends. Once your firm becomes a comfortable family, huddled in fancy digs, it will decline.

CHAPTER EIGHT

Know Yourself

My colleague in New York City runs a CEO roundtable. Her chief executives meet monthly to discuss their corporate challenges and exchange ideas for resolving them.

Her biggest challenge? Recruiting them. You read that correctly. It takes my colleague almost a year to coax into the fold each CEO, who, typically, is loath to discuss openly his flaws, foibles, and failures.

Believe it or not, these CEOs need a safespace.

The fear of publicly admitting mistakes explains why many CEOs dismiss branding: the unsafe, public declaration of a value proposition, *driver of all other corporate functions.*

To requote Andy Warhol (see Chapter One): "The moment you label something, you take a step. I mean, you can never go back again to seeing it unlabeled."

Translation: *there's no place to hide.*

I'll paraphrase the paragraph above, lest you missed, or dismissed, it: *All other corporate functions are subordinate to the brand* (see Chapter One).

Here's some insight: that statement is heretical in branding-phobic, product-centric precincts like Silicon Valley.

Speaking of Silicon Valley, there's a "pivot" culture in this insular techdom, courtesy of VCs (venture capitalists), that violates branding principles.

The philosophy is: If startup companies hit brick walls, they can pivot to totally new companies, with different reasons for being—just like that. This alters attitudes and behaviors.

To wit: Why, then, would any startup CEO in Silicon Valley *not* dismiss branding?

Pivoting is the penalty for *not* branding first, **before** designing your product. Pivoting raises your costs of sales, capital, and media—and wastes time. Avoid this setback.

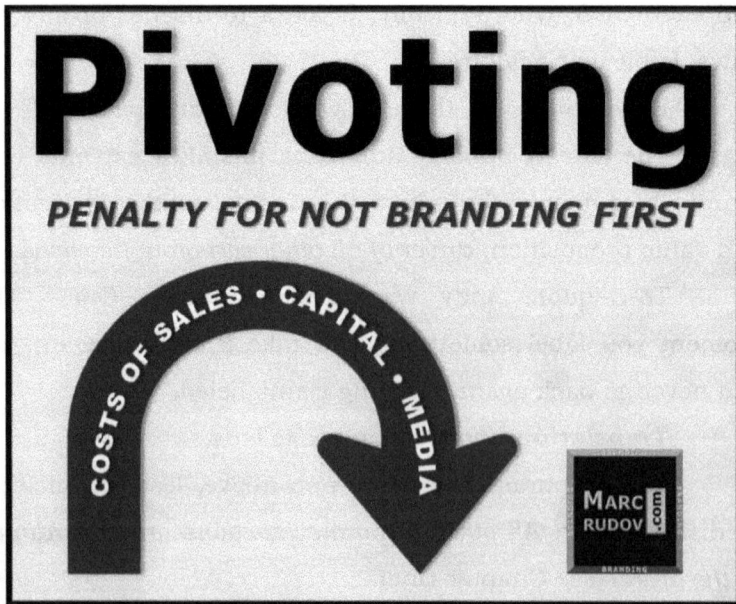

As we discussed in Chapter Seven, a brand is akin to a GPS system's input: without said input, the enterprise has no identifiable destiny and no clear itinerary. Yahoo, which is imploding, is a perfect example.

CEOs habitually stuff their branding vacuums with hailstorms of new products and technologies, hoping one of them will stick. This behavior is cultural.

Alas, this chaotic paradigm renders each product a fiefdom unto itself, in search of customers, with its own messaging. Such is an obvious disaster, redolent of the one Yahoo's CEO, Marissa Mayer, created by trying to fix a broken, brandless company with products and technologies.

Fear of Branding

Your company *must* have a single brand—not multiple product fiefdoms and messages. Yes, this means putting all your eggs in one branding basket, without hedging and waffling and hiding behind industry jargon. Risky. Unsafe.

In Chapter Seven of *Be Unique or Be Ignored*, I wrote about the CEO's fear of branding. Here's a snippet:

> As a "blender" CEO, you're likely to veto a brilliant branding idea because it isn't *your* style, not something *you* would create—and it makes *you* uncomfortable. Your veto could cost your company millions in lost opportunities. Better idea: *veto your discomfort.*

How does fear of branding manifest in your company? People inhabit one of three zones: comfort, indecision, and discomfort.

In the figure below, we see that the *comfort zone*, AKA Jargonville, is where the blenders live. It is the smallest of the three zones, because people have small comfort zones.

The next zone is for *indecision*. Notice that people, to feel "safe," vacillate between comfort and indecision. When push comes to shove, they'll revert to comfort. They love that nobody-will-fire-me-for-using-jargon feeling.

Finally, we arrive at the *discomfort zone*, Uniqueville, where real branders live. It's the largest because most people have lots of fears and avoid treading here. Hire those who don't fear this zone; *listen to them, even if they're not like you.*

Elizabeth Bernstein wrote a perceptive piece in the *Wall Street Journal* about the different styles of introverted vs. extroverted CEOs, save one component: no explanation of the effect of personality on *branding.* No surprise: most CEOs don't understand branding and its significance to sustainable corporate success (destiny).

Bernstein made the following personality observations:

- Extroverts comprise 60% of top executives
- Introverts aren't looking for outside events to validate their plans—or themselves
- Extroverts can get sidetracked by seeking external validation, such as awards or media attention for a project.

Introverts err by *not* seeking outside events to validate their plans. This is a case of sheer hubris or deep insecurity, or both. Without external validation, there is no brand.

Self-validation, as opposed to brand validation, is pure narcissism and meaningless to branding—and that's where extroverts like Donald Trump can go sideways.

Note: Branding is about connecting with buyers, not about products, companies, technologies, or egos.

Whether extrovert or introvert, you must jettison your insecurities and your hubris, and be aware of why you did so.

Branding 101 requires your company to make a bold, unique, public promise to customers, *and then live up to it.* In other words, walk your talk. So, ensure that *your* personality doesn't distort or damage your enterprise's personality.

CEOs dismiss and fear branding for three reasons: they don't understand it, it's beneath them, or it makes them uncomfortable. All three are related to personality.

There's no excuse in any of these cases: Branding is the #1 priority. I won't stop repeating it.

Disrupt your old thinking.

I was describing to a CEO my first book on branding, *Be Unique or Be Ignored*, specifically my claim in the Preface that most CEOs don't care about branding.

His response: "That's true. I don't give a shit about it. I just sell." He was quite proud of that proclamation.

"What do you tell customers when you sell?" I asked. "I'm not sure, but whatever it is, it seems to work," he quipped.

How can he train his salesforce?

Imagine all your employees, in all your departments, winging it like that and being so undisciplined! Your behavior and speech set the tone. You can create a Tower of Babel.

Mandate the discipline of branding throughout the ranks of your firm. Every employee must be able to recite its brand, easily and reflexively—or you're running an entroprise.

CEO's Top Sales Tool

When I mention "branding" to the typical CEO, it's as though I've uttered *colonoscopy*. He'll cringe, squirm, and exclaim, *We did that last year and are good for a while.*

To dismiss branding is to reject sales and customers. Branding and selling and customers are inextricably linked.

I once lectured a room full of young entrepreneurs, the majority of whom were building unfathomable social-media products. They were seeking investment capital and wanted to learn about messaging, a synonym for branding.

Prior to standing before them, I sat in the audience, listening to their pitches. One by one, these entrepreneurs tried to explain why their creations would be popular, based on the premise that *anything* in the social media space would be popular.

All I did was scratch my head. Not one of these ideas seemed the least bit practical or necessary. The would-be CEOs were following, not decoding, the social-media trend.

Then, it was my turn. I gave them my Branding 101 presentation. I knew that none of them had ever heard such concepts, as they were accustomed to watching technology evangelists wave their pompoms.

To take the audience's temperature, I needed some coordinates. "How many of you have sold at high levels in corporations?" I inquired. Zero responses. "How many of you have ever sold *anything*?" I persisted. Again, zero responses.

I was astonished, dumbfounded. But, the revelation made sense. In my experience, builders of products tend to be myopically focused on themselves—and on nuts and bolts—not on customers and *their* needs.

I told them that, without knowing how to navigate the management structures of small and large corporations, they never would learn how to locate the real decisionmakers and influencers, get feedback on their ideas, and build and hone their persuasion skills. Blank stares.

Chalk this up to living in artificial social media.

Selling teaches people to listen and perceive. One who never has sold anything before won't know the art of listening.

The probability is small that a CEO bereft of face-to-face sales and negotiating experience will grasp customers' needs and wants, then conceive and grow a firm that sells desirable, profitable products over a long period.

Without selling experience, branding won't be on your agenda—or in your vernacular. Your costs of sales, capital, and media, in turn, will be needlessly high.

Incidentally, when I post about this topic of CEOs and "listening" on Twitter, accompanied by the graphic below, I lose followers. Always. Sometimes 20 in a short span.

Why?

Because the snowflakes on Twitter get butt-hurt easily and often, especially when a topic contradicts their long-held beliefs. Any suggestion that technology does not solve every problem offends a lot of snowflakes. I'm not kidding.

Your top sales—*and branding*—tool, hence, is your *ear*, forever trained on the voice of the customer. With your ear, you can hear—*and you must do so in real conversations with real customers, in front of them, as often as possible.*

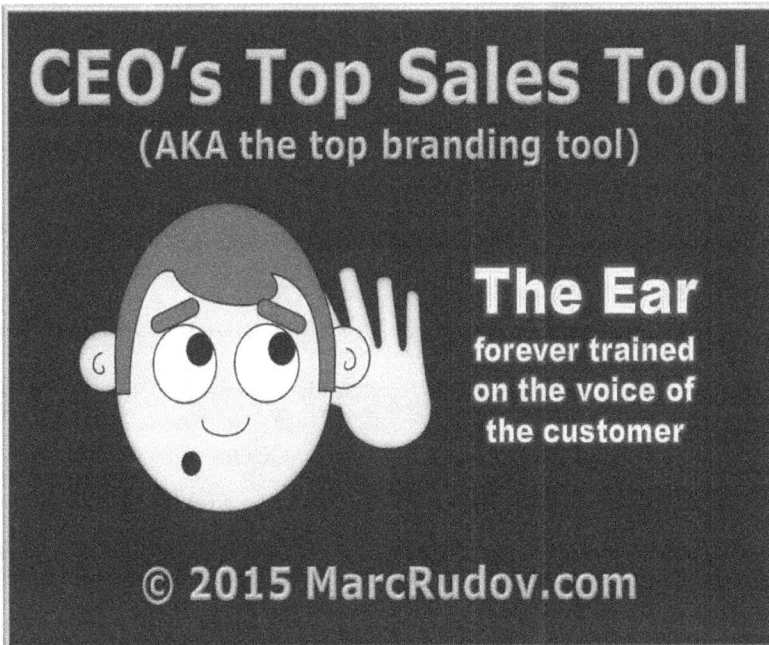

Reading Twitter and Facebook posts is *not* tantamount to having your ear trained on the voice of the customer. Without your ear, live in fear that your company's destiny is imperiled—as was the case for McDonald's.

McDonald's was rapidly sinking into oblivion: it had violated Branding 101 by ignoring its core customers and trying to become a healthfood chain for Millennials.

For years, McDonald's customers had clamored for all-day breakfast, to no avail. The company's CEOs and top execs had ignored them and the store managers advocating it.

Along came a new CEO, Steve Easterbrook, who saw the declining sales and defecting franchisees. He used his ear and then posited a novel idea: *heed our customers!*

McD's now serves all-day breakfast; sales are climbing.

Yes, McDonald's saved itself with all-day breakfast. Actually, it saved itself with all-day *branding.* McD's collective ear, under a new CEO, is now trained on the voice of the customer. *The strongest brand always wins.*

Technology Obsession

PwC's 2016 annual survey of CEOs reflects a top-10 concern about technology needed to "establish a flexible and secure foundation for delivering the services and experiences that will set them apart."

As we learned in the "Cordcutter" and "Nike" sections of Chapter Three, technology is not a replacement for building trust with your customers. Technology is a means to an end, *not* the end—and that end is a strong brand.

Never think of or use technology as a panacea to paper over problems that your company's attitude, strategy, and behaviors cause—or overlook.

Knowing yourself will help you determine when and where technology helps and hurts your company's ability to reach its destiny.

CHAPTER NINE

Unsocial Media

In my extensive experience, social media (SM) are good for three activities: hyping, sniping, and griping—*but terrible for branding and selling.*

In a *Wall Street Journal* article, on December 26, 2016, bankruptcy lawyers discussed the futility of using SM to bust alleged criminals purportedly hiding assets:

> *The industry's detectives—lawyers and accountants who serve as chapter 7 bankruptcy trustees—are learning what most teenagers have already figured out, which is that you can't always believe what you see on Facebook and Twitter.*
>
> *"Gotcha" moments in which they discover people in bankruptcy posing in glamorous-looking jewelry, piloting boats and ATVs, and even displaying buckets full of cash have fallen flat as the items turn out to be fake, or not theirs at all.*

Last month, a New Mexico trustee was questioning a bankrupt man about his hobbies, pushing him to discuss his fishing gear and identify his preferred brands, says the bankrupt man's lawyer, Michael Daniels. The impatient trustee finally snapped, "You were using a much nicer reel on your Facebook page!" Mr. Daniels recalls.

The man replied that he had borrowed gear for the shot.

You've got to use [social media] with a grain of salt," says Mr. Daniels.

Fun Facts

Use social media with a grain of salt. Sage advice. But, do you hear such comments in corporate America? Nope. The largest firms, to be technologically correct, are committed to social media and digital advertising—despite the facts:

60 percent of Twitter's 320M active users never read the tweets they share with others;

Per the Association of National Advertisers, in 2016, marketers wasted about $7B on online ads that 80 percent of people didn't even see—because of fake Web traffic generated by "bots": computer programs that mimic human mouse movements and clicks to give the impression that a person is visiting a website;

Facebook disclosed, in November 2016, that it had overstated its ad metric for counting referral traffic by six percent and overstated time spent on stories by seven to eight percent;

In June 2016, Russian hackers breached 33M Twitter accounts and posted the passwords on "the dark web," a service that requires special software to access;

According to Gallup, 62 percent of US adults who use social media say these sites have *no influence* on their purchasing decisions and only 5 percent say they have a great deal of influence;

According to McKinsey, companies have devoted more time and money for gaining new customers to social networks and 20 percent less to e-mail, *even though e-mail is nearly 40 times more effective than Facebook and Twitter combined*;

Harvard Business Review concluded, in 2015, that social media *do NOT* help your company's bottom line.

Likaholics

Unfortunately, most executives insisting that their companies "be social" are personally unfamiliar with using social media. Otherwise, they'd stop it.

Fortunately, I *am* familiar with the social media. Using them for business is laughable (hyping, sniping, and griping).

Think about it: Do social and business mix? Go to a party. Start pitching your product. You'll be a pariah. The name "social" is your first clue about SM's ineffectiveness.

One of the odd SM characters is the *likaholic,* someone literally hooked on "liking" posts. For the life of me, I don't get this person.

For example, I'll post on Twitter my latest branding video (typically 4-10 minutes long). Within *30 seconds,* "likes" start appearing. Yet, not one likaholic has viewed, or will view, my video. That's the point: likaholics just like to "like"—and *don't even know what they're liking.* Getting the picture?

In addition to liking, people reflexively retweet posts: they tweet others' posts, so their own followers can see them. Often, a Twitter user's profile includes this caveat: *Retweets (RTs) are not endorsements.* If not, why rebroadcast them?

Twitter also allows one user to add other users to self-created lists, arranged by category. Example: I'll tweet a post with the hashtag #PrivateEquity. Users will add me to their PE lists but never call or write to me. Why? Useless nonsense.

Twitter allows users to message each other directly, via Twitter, with a direct message (DM). Some vendor will follow me. If I believe this company could become a client, I'll follow it back. Then, I'll get an *anonymous* DM about how wonderful this firm is and why I should be excited. I'll reply this way: *Thanks for writing. Please identify yourself and your title, and tell me what you find interesting about me and my branding practice.* No subsequent response, ever. This is typical.

Finally, we have copycat networks. I'm on LinkedIn. I'll get invitations from people on AngelList, a site for startups in search of capital from angels: wealthy individuals who invest hundreds of thousands of dollars in seed funding.

Every time I get an invitation, I discover we're *already connected on LinkedIn.* Why yet another network? It's stupid. I think to myself, *If you're so interested in me, call.*

One day, I got pissed. I called an exec in New Jersey, already connected to me on LinkedIn, who had invited me to AngelList. We'd never spoken. "If you're *that* interested, why didn't you call me?" I pressed. Her reply: "Oh, I invite people just to do it, without thinking. I like to expand my networks."

This is a total waste of your firm's time and money. It's a bunch of people who haven't the balls or the reason to call each other but prefer instead a **click-to-feel-busy** existence.

Fire Your Hashtaggers

You're a CEO. Critical question: *Would you send poor communicators to meet with your best client?* Not if you're a good CEO. Why, then, put them on your branding team?

If you employ hashtaggers—those who create dopey hashtagged slogans for Twitter—fire them, whether they be employees or ad-agency contractors.

Poor communicators are branding bozos, drivers of high sales, capital, and media costs. Why do you hire them? Answer: you're copying your competitors. As I conveyed to you numerous times, imitating is blending, *not* branding.

The hashtag, a specifically descriptive term preceded by the # sign, was originally designed to funnel tweets to other users with common interests (such as #PrivateEquity in the previous section). It has devolved into fatuous jargon.

In today's chaotic Twitterverse, the hashtag's an inane, useless phrase, with a half-life of 10 minutes, that branding bozos use to "communicate" with Twitter hipsters.

As we learned in the "Virtue Signaling" section of Chapter Four, people also use the hashtag to convey moral superiority, to soothe their own egos.

The hashtag is now an out-of-control replacement for competent communication. Incessant, indiscriminate hashtag usage signals *branding ineptitude.*

Do you want customers to buy and recommend your product, or get pissed off deciphering your latest hashtag?

You'd be surprised how many never thought of this or, worse, don't give a crap. Trendiness supersedes effectiveness.

Not only do hashtags *not* attract customers to your brand and company, they do the *opposite*.

If you've approved this hashtag horseshit, read some of your ad copy. Ask yourself, **What is our company's brand?**

In a fatuous Walmart commercial, which was pitching Straight Talk mobile service, the salesrep (see photo, center) inundated the husband and wife with facts and prices. Husband reacts: "#LotsOfOptions." Wife reacts: "#Awesome." Husband, again: "#Hashtag (really)." Upshot: Inept waste of shareholder cash, in the name of attracting Millennials.

Customers *aren't* employees. They *don't* work for you. Stop making them work to buy your products.

Social Mediapathy

When talking to my business colleagues, in every quarter, I hear a common complaint: *There's a general paucity of civility and courtesy in daily discourse and commerce.*

To wit: People no longer feel obligated to return phone calls and respond to emails—either in a timely manner or at all—and, in general, extend any social graces.

It's the new norm, and those of us who detest it feel helpless to fix it. In fact, they begrudgingly tolerate it.

There was a time in our society, not so long ago, when such boorish conduct would result in getting one ostracized and shunned.

No more. The overt check on public shaming is gone.

But, there *is* a cost. Aloof boors unwittingly devalue their companies' brands and themselves—as some ignored parties harbor *silent* resentment, retaliate anonymously, and shop elsewhere. Others openly trash you on social media.

Pretending this isn't true will worsen the situation and damage your brand, destiny, and bottom line. Take this seriously. Don't permit it.

Given the repercussions, why the boorish behavior? Are the boors too busy or unaware of the consequences?

No, they don't care enough to recognize or grasp their own insulting behavior or its consequences.

Chalk it up to an *apathetic* culture, derived from three intertwined causes:

Big Government: massive statist programs and control have replaced the tradition of people helping themselves and each other: they now know, think, feel, and do less than their forebears. Whenever a problem arises in society, here's the first response: *We need new legislation to fix it.* No more independent, critical thinking and self-reliance.

Infantilization: Millennials' demands for safespaces, even at their jobs, indicates a pervasive immaturity. Originating at universities, which prohibit "offensive" speech and Halloween costumes, it has infected the larger population. Ironically, the snowflakes who seek protection from "pain" are the first to inflict it, unfeelingly, on others; that's why cosseted college students bully those whose ideas differ from theirs. The safespace tyranny is so severe, NYU suspended a professor who railed against it.

Unsocial media: digital destinations like Facebook, Twitter, LinkedIn, YouTube, Instagram, Buzzfeed, and Snapchat. I characterize them as "unsocial" because they've rendered their users rude, crude, vile, inept, passive-aggressive, and detached.

Writing in the April 2017 issue of *Computers in Human Behavior*, researchers from the University of Pittsburgh Center for Research on Media, Technology, and Health conclude that young adults who use seven or more social-media platforms are *three times* more likely to develop depression and anxiety than those who use between zero and two platforms.

Spending time on unsocial media, akin to submerging oneself in a sensory-deprivation tank, leaves one isolated and desensitized—unable to perceive, feel, and communicate with real human beings.

I call this callous condition *social mediapathy* **(mee-dee-APP-uh-thee).**

There's a double entendre at play here. Apathy means lack of feeling, which today is rampant and ubiquitous. The suffix "pathy" connotes disease or disorder (e.g., neuropathy: damaged nerves). *We have a damaged culture.*

Why should you care about social mediapathy? It fosters callousness, contempt, and condescension in your ranks, affecting how they treat customers and each other.

Anthony Bourdain, host of *Parts Unknown* on CNN, observed to *Reason* magazine, in December 2016, how badly East Coast elitists regard and treat regular folks:

> *"The utter contempt with which privileged Eastern liberals such as myself discuss red-state, gun-country, working-class America as ridiculous and morons and rubes is largely responsible for the upswell of rage and contempt and desire to pull down the temple that we're seeing now.*
>
> *"The self-congratulatory tone of the privileged left—just repeating and repeating and repeating the outrages of*

the opposition—this does not win hearts and minds. It doesn't change anyone's opinions. It only solidifies them, and makes things worse for all of us."

Branding is predicated on appealing to and conveying *adult* emotions. Alas, it's tough to conceive and execute a successful branding strategy—*when its disdainful authors cosset helpless snowflakes and insult everyone else.*

The dearth of common sense necessarily accompanies and exacerbates the detached use of unsocial media, the death of critical thinking, and the death of self-reliance.

Man-in-the-street interviews continuously reveal how little Americans know or *care* about history, current events (other than the latest Kardashian crap), and civics—despite having a cornucopia of information at their fingertips.

It's likely that your company *heavily depends* on unsocial media, AKA the sensory-deprivation tank. *Terminate this lousy strategy.* Use unsocial media sparingly and only in ways *supplementary* to your core activities, period.

Use email, the telephone, face-to-face selling, and tradeshows to establish direct, personal relationships with customers and prospects you can engage and verify.

Conquer social mediapathy by acknowledging it and refusing to tolerate and perpetuate it. Force employees to feel, to think, to cope. Ban all safespaces: Life is tough.

Be an example of responsiveness. Fire employees who refuse to respond quickly to phone calls and emails. Restore civility and courtesy in daily discourse and commerce.

Donald Trump Exception

Many pundits are marveling over Donald Trump's use of Twitter, and how he circumvents the dishonest traditional media to take his messages, unfiltered, directly to Americans. They advocate that all businesses and politicians should copy Trump's social-media strategy and tactics. *Don't do it.*

Donald Trump is the exception, not the rule.

Before entering the presidential race in June 2015, Mr. Trump already was a famous celebrity, and a newsmaking provocateur at that.

More important, Trump adeptly gained his fame using *traditional* media—radio, TV, books, movies, magazines, and newspapers—to trumpet his activities, achievements, attacks on others, and persona.

Remember: Without his previously earned fame and celebrity, Donald Trump would *not* have been able to use social media to ignore and bypass the established media.

Bottom Line

Social media are unsocial, artificial, offputting, noisy, undependable conduits for hyping, sniping, and griping—and *not* good for connecting, branding, and selling.

Unsocial media inspire and encourage dysfunctional behavior, not conducive to commerce.

Never design your company to *depend* on unsocial media. You'll jeopardize your destiny and bottom line.

CHAPTER TEN

Disruption Distraction

In the panoply of perpetual panaceas, *disruption* is the latest boardroom obsession—whether it's needed or not.

Such tunnel vision reminds of a clever song Groucho Marx sang in the 1932 Marx Brothers classic movie, *Horse Feathers.* Here's the first verse:

> *I don't know what they have to say;*
> *It makes no difference anyway;*
> *Whatever it is, I'm against it!*
> *No matter what it is,*
> *Or who commenced it,*
> *I'm against it!*

That's how disruption is myopically discussed today. No matter your company's problem, disruption is the answer. This is patently absurd and a distraction from branding.

Gurus, books, articles, speeches, videos, and seminars abound, admonishing CEOs to "disrupt" (abruptly shake up) their companies and marketplaces before competitors, fads, or trends—*real or perceived*—beat them to it.

Alas, in our "follower" culture, where critical thinking is rarely demanded, or employed, blind conformity trumps buzzword skepticism.

What is disruption? Is disruption for you? How do you know? The answer always depends on the problem and its severity. Amputate a leg to cure a headache? I doubt it.

Visualize an unruly child disrupting a classroom, a cheating spouse disrupting a marriage. Is that what *you* want in your organization? It's tough to manage your firm, even in the best of times. Would you prefer that your enterprise become a chaotic entroprise?

CEOs must question *why* they should interrupt their employees, disturb their customers, and fundamentally and abruptly transform their value propositions.

Disruption has a cost. People hate and resist big changes, which, in most cases, are completely unnecessary.

Let's say, while driving or flying to a destination, the driver or pilot realizes he's off-course (a perfect metaphor for corporate life).

Would he react by slamming on the brakes and hooking an abrupt u-turn—thereby smashing his passengers' faces against the windows?

No, he would make a sequence of incremental course corrections—*tweaks*—to reverse the mistake.

Now, if the driver is being chased by an armed murderer, or the pilot by an enemy fighter, he'll do *whatever is necessary* to survive—including sudden braking and abrupt u-turns. When a CEO's job is to save a company from near-extinction, disruption is mandatory. *Otherwise, it is not.*

Also, if disruption is required, it is *not* a one-size-fits-all remedy, despite what cheerleaders and zealots advocate. Like everything else in life, it depends.

The CEO must assess her corporate vector to determine whether gutwrenching disruption is the right or wrong course correction.

Specifically, is her company growing, spinning (going nowhere), or shrinking. Why and to what extent? Knowing the answers is crucial before acting.

Frequently, the fix is easy, painless, and cheap—killing a product, firing an executive, reorganizing a department, or improving the attitude. But, by ignoring the problem long enough, the fix will be painful, expensive, and maybe moot.

![Corporate Vectors. Three icons: an upward arrow labeled "Growing", a circular arrow labeled "Spinning", and a downward arrow labeled "Shrinking". © 2015 MarcRudov.com](image)

In *Be Unique or Be Ignored,* I reported that former JC Penney CEO, Ron Johnson, almost killed the old retailer by brashly disrupting it. Penney's current CEO, Marvin Ellison, is *growing* the company—*by testing and tweaking programs.*

Ellison told *Fortune* in February 2016 that *small but meaningful* improvements will add up to a full recovery, and Penney's growth will come from getting a lot more sales from its existing customers. Johnson, on the other hand, tried to replace Penney's customer base, overnight. It was a disaster.

As I noted in the "Cordcutters" section of Chapter Three, the cable companies now are scrambling to keep subscribers, *because they refused to make the easy tweaks a long time ago.* But, to paraphrase Groucho Marx, the usual zealots are shouting, in panic, "Whatever it is, disrupt it."

Bottom Line

One of my axioms: *The cost of panic greatly exceeds the cost of preparation. Alas, many are willing to pay that price.*

Don't pay that price. Prepare. And, if your enterprise is not imploding, disruption is *not* for you.

Your course correction, hence, should be incremental, immediate, and incessant. And, it must include aligning your brand and destiny.

Never put your employees and customers through needless, preventable, costly turmoil and upheaval.

Finally, if disruption *is* for you, branding has *not* been for you and *not* your priority. **Don't repeat that mistake.**

CHAPTER ELEVEN

The Inflated Entrepreneur

People are cursed with the infatuation gene. When strong emotions blind them, they inflate the values of cars, homes, tulip bulbs (in 1637 Holland), stocks, other people—and, of course, technology—resulting in illogical overpayments that they later regret.

Widespread overpayments cause bubbles, which eventually burst, along with prices. The aftermath is always the same, when the victims ask, *How did this happen?*

We're experiencing yet another tech bubble. Utopian unicorn-chasers—evangelists, engineers, investors, reporters, and seminar hucksters—believe that technology solves all problems, real and imagined.

By the way, a "unicorn" is a private company valued at $1B or more.

I have pet names for their "religious" zeal: *technologism* and *technologica erotica*. These are not the emotions of people who want to solve business problems but of those who seek validation and desire self-approval by "changing the world."

Technologism is reflected in thousands of help-wanted ads, appearing daily on every imaginable employment site, in search of marketing folks afflicted with technologica erotica.

HELP WANTED

Seeking Marketing Professional, ASAP

You must love technology, especially wireless...

Newsflash: Technologism and branding are mutually exclusive. Customers buy *value*, not technology. So, if your company engages in this nonsense, *cease the practice at once.*

Branding and marketing professionals must focus on customers and have expertise in communicating with them— not be *predisposed* to faddish agendas or product categories, *before* diagnosing customers' problems and needs.

Technology doesn't solve all problems, often creates them, and can be silly. Frequently, common sense solves more than elaborate software and hardware ever could.

Example: People are so dumb, apparently, they can't figure out when to drink water. A group of students at the University of Minnesota created a "smart" water bottle, called HidrateMe, to do just that. The $45 product has an internal sensor that tracks and directs water intake, and transmits that data, via Bluetooth, to the owner's phone. This startup raised over $450K on Kickstarter; then, it joined the Sprint Mobile Health Accelerator Program.

When investors fund ridiculous companies like this one, and inflate their valuations, voila, they create a bubble comprised of similar companies and products that never should see the light of day.

Do you need a smartphone app to admonish you to lose weight? You can download several. What happened to the full-length mirror, the belt, ill-fitting pants, and the bathroom scale? Are these time-tested indicators too easy?

Insane valuations of tech startups abound. Stewart Butterfield, cofounder of Flickr and now CEO of software purveyor Slack, opined to Sarah Lacy at a San Francisco conference in March 2015: "It's arbitrary as fuck. There's no logic to what you get valued at."

Concurrently, Bloomberg BusinessWeek wrote this: "Here's the secret to how Silicon Valley calculates the value of its hottest companies: The numbers are sort of made-up."

As I cited in *Be Unique or Be Ignored*, 75% of startups fail. Why wouldn't they fail? They worship products and technologies and fads—instead of customers—thereby sealing their fateful destinies.

For starters, blame venture-capital firms (VCs), which back and hypervalue startups.

The typical VC firm is itself organized by technologies looking for homes (versus problems that need solving), and actively preaches and promulgates technologism—and, in the process, creates bubbles, or what I call techflation.

Missing in the equation: risk, the universal clarifier.

VCs can make many bad investments in startups, yet continue to receive tranches of funds from equally zealous foundations, insurance carriers, universities, and pensions.

Investors in and founders of startups risk almost none of their own cash and can exit unscathed from failed ones.

Without risk and the cloud of failure and personal loss hanging over the heads of founders and investors, branding—*precise customer targeting and connection, verified product utility, and purchase validation*—isn't a priority.

If that's the case, why not, then, like HidrateMe, build more superfluous gadgets for fun, glory, and adventure? It's happening, and I submit that the perps are tinkerers (who build products), not entrepreneurs (who solve problems)!

Entrepreneur or Tinkerer?

What problem can I solve?

What product can I build?

E

T

Be Unique or Be Ignored.com

Aiding the VCs are the sycophantic media, which are constantly hyping tech products, tech firms, and tech CEOs—instead of skeptically analyzing them.

It's not just TechCrunch, *Wired*, and *CIO*. Mainstream business pubs—*Bloomberg BusinessWeek, Fortune, Forbes, The Wall Street Journal, Financial Times*—are equally guilty.

Recent hyping examples are the Apple Watch, GoPro, Hampton Creek, and Theranos. Why advertise when giddy journos and their organs will campaign for you. Why, indeed.

The VCs and media can't perpetuate technologism and techflation without the vaunted entrepreneur. Together, they incestuously form the Tech-VC-Media Complex, which, unchecked, effects the build-fund-hype cycle that spawns unicorns and bubbles.

Technologism
Tech/VC/Media Complex
BUILD
HYPE
FUND
Technologica Erotica
© 2017 MarcRudov.com

Where's the critical thinking, the skepticism, the hard digging? Nonexistent in the fog of technologism.

Because of this culture of veneration, an endless line of inflated entrepreneurs and revered hobbyists who build cool stuff, or talk a good game, get investment funding.

Celebrating Failure

Erin Griffith wrote an amazing piece in the 12/28/16 issue of *Fortune,* called "The Ugly Unethical Underside of Silicon Valley." Here are two excerpted paragraphs:

> *The drama has some investors predicting more disasters. "What if Theranos is the canary in the coal mine?" says Roger McNamee, a 40-year VC veteran and managing director at Elevation Partners. "Everyone is looking at Theranos as an outlier. We may discover it's not an outlier at all." That would be bad news, because without trust, the tech industry's intertwined ecosystem of money, products, and people can't function. Investors may find the full version of the old proverb is more accurate: "One bad apple spoils the whole barrel."*

> *Historically, Silicon Valley forgives, even celebrates, failure. E-commerce startup Fab.com promised world domination, then promptly burned through $336 million of investors' money, selling for just $15 million. That didn't stop some of the same investors from giving millions to cofounders Jason Goldberg and Bradford*

Shellhammer for their next startups (Shellhammer's failed in less than a year). Zenefits CEO Parker Conrad stepped down amid the cheating scandal in February; within months he was working on a new employee-benefits startup that sounds a lot like Zenefits. It helps if you spin your meltdown as a learning experience.

If the aforementioned doesn't give you pause, nothing will. In Silicon Valley's see-no-evil culture, you can see why branding takes a backseat. *In fact, it's not even in the car.*

What Is an Entrepreneur?

This begs the question: What is an entrepreneur? It's someone who takes *risk*, especially financial risk, to create and run a company that provides a *unique, customer-validated solution to a real problem.*

> **Scenario A:** *A man buys the corner dry-cleaner shop with a small percentage down. He takes over the expenses and pays the seller the purchase balance, in installments, from a guaranteed revenue stream.*

Is he an entrepreneur? Absolutely not. A proprietor, yes. Entrepreneur, no. Nothing new and unique. No risk. Is he called an entrepreneur? Yes. Does he consider himself an entrepreneur? Probably. Are investors beating down his door to motivate him to buy similar businesses? Perhaps. Will the media hype him or his company? No.

> **Scenario B:** *A woman moves into an incubator, where she gets free office space, amenities, and access to a free CPA, a free lawyer, and free selling advice. She builds a product, based on super-cool technology, which solves no real problem. She's under no pressure. She can't articulate a clear, concise, compelling message— but nobody cares.*

Is she an entrepreneur? Absolutely not: no risk, no unique solution to a real problem, no brand. Is she called an entrepreneur? Absolutely. Does she consider herself an entrepreneur? Yes. Will VCs clamor to fund her? Yes. Will the media hype her and her product? Yes, especially because she is a *she*. In many precincts, diversity trumps meritocracy.

Incubators have become riskless sandboxes for tinkerers, under the inflated ruse of entrepreneurship. They foster a plethora of products in search of problems—most of which will be massive wastes of time and capital: *83%* of the 1.42M apps in Apple's App Store don't sell.

Bottom Line

Don't self-inflate. Become a real entrepreneur, not a tinkerer. Take risks. Create a company, with a strong brand, that solves a *real* problem—not one in your imagination.

Bubbles, derived from infatuation, make hazardous, unprofitable destinies. Eventually, they deflate or pop. Never, ever create or inhabit one.

CHAPTER TWELVE

Branding Healthcare

The latest buzzword to circulate the medical world, especially in the wake of that disaster known as Obamacare, is value-based healthcare, or VBC.

Value, *not* products, services, or technologies, is what customers and medical patients want to purchase. Branding is about creating, articulating, and delivering *value*.

Traditionally, healthcare has revolved around fee-for-service, wherein doctors, hospitals, and clinics get paid based on the *number and kind* of tests and procedures they deliver, *not* on whether patients are satisfied and healthy afterwards.

Unfortunately, traditional healthcare has resulted in escalating costs and inconsistent quality, leaving consumers little power to know or optimize their limited options.

Kathleen Sebelius was secretary of Health and Human Services during the bungled Obamacare launch. Her IT hacks spent $1B on the Healthcare.gov rollout—and it still didn't work. Despite the hoopla, healthy Millennials, who were needed to subsidize the unhealthy, weren't signing up.

On December 10, 2014, Ms. Sebelius told *Politico*: "Obamacare has a very bad brand. I think we may need to call it something in the future different, but it's working."

Working? What an amateurish, cynical comment. A brand is a *value* proposition, not a name. Failure isn't value. Renaming the sinking Titanic wouldn't have saved it.

Obamacare was designed to fail, to be the antithesis of patient-centricity, and to be forced on the American public. Not one Republican voted for it. Jonathan Gruber, MIT economist and Obamacare architect, was videotaped bragging, to a private audience, that passing Obamacare required a lack of transparency to fool the stupid American voters.

President Obama promised the American people that, under Obamacare, if they liked their then-current doctors and plans, they could keep both, and that premiums would drop by $2,500 per family. All untrue.

Obamacare is "working" so well that: during 2016, the number of doctors accepting its "insured" dropped by 20 percent; Aetna and United Healthcare exited the business; and premiums rose by an average of 25 percent (145 percent in Phoenix). Deductibles for individuals enrolled in the *lowest-priced* plans will average more than $6,000 in 2017.

In a rare moment of candor, Bill Clinton, in October 2016, while campaigning for his wife, opined thusly:

> *You've got this crazy system where, all of a sudden, 25 million more people have healthcare and then the people are out there busting it, sometimes 60 hours a week,*

wind up with their premiums doubled and their
coverage cut in half. It's the craziest thing in the world.
The people that are getting killed in this deal are small
businesspeople and individuals who make just a little
too much to get any of these subsidies.

President Donald Trump has promised to repeal and replace Obamacare—to give patients, not bureaucrats and insurance companies, the power to determine the care they get, where they get it, and how much they'll pay for it.

When this happens, it will mark a huge change from the current patient experience: feeling like a manila folder, draped in an ill-fitting hospital gown, sitting on (or bending over) a white-papered examination table, fearing that the doctor may be too incompetent or too busy to care, and not knowing how financially crippling the final invoice will be.

Medicare, America's largest health insurer, dictates the amounts hospitals currently charge for procedures, tests, bandages, and medications—and the amounts insurers will reimburse for same. Based on what? Few people know. These amounts, for sure, aren't based on real costs or value.

There are many academic proposals for "disrupting" the current system: injecting more technology into the mix, integrating care from unrelated providers, and standardizing the "measurement of outcomes," to name a few.

These ideas warm the heart. But, the best way to fix this fiasco is to remove the government and shift the epicenter from provider to patient, who judges value for himself.

The patient-customer should have a portable health savings account (HSA) and the freedom to shop anywhere for his preferred carriers, plans, hospitals, and doctors.

The best way to achieve this is with a tried-and-true system: *free enterprise.* Accordingly, a California resident would be free to purchase a customized, affordable policy—as *he* defines that—from, say, an insurance firm in New Jersey.

Currently, insurance firms in each state are protected from interstate competition by the federal McCarran-Ferguson Act of 1945, which grants states the right to regulate health plans within their borders. It's time to repeal this law.

Large employers that self-insure (500+ employees) are exempt from these state regulations and under the auspices of the federal ERISA law, enforced by the US Department of Labor. Result: 50 different sets of state regulations. Nonsense.

Bottom Line

Branding healthcare will succeed *only* if the patient-consumers get the value they want, as *they* define it.

Ergo, those conceiving and competing to deliver value-based care *must* eradicate uneconomic laws, regulations, taxes, and, thus, profit-killing compliance departments.

Finally, unless hospital and clinic CEOs weaken trade and labor unions—*which impede change, inflate costs, and deflate staffers, who typically think and care more about their hours, benefits, and grievances than satisfying customers and beating competitors*—all attempts to fix healthcare will fail.

CHAPTER THIRTEEN

Sears: Leader to Loser

Sears was once America's largest retailer, until the rocket called Walmart surpassed it in October 1989. Sadly, Sears squandered its once-solid brand—effecting a perilous destiny and thereby smashing its bottom line.

As 2016 drew to a close, Sears Holdings, which owns both Sears and Kmart, reported a $748 million net loss and an adjusted third-quarter loss of $333 million. It announced a desire to sell its Kenmore (appliances), Craftsman (tools), and DieHard (car batteries) labels.

Then, on January 5, 2017, Sears Holdings announced the closing of 150 stores and the sale of the Craftsman label, for $900 million, to Stanley Black & Decker. Sears can license the Craftsman name, royalty-free, for 15 years after the deal closes. Here's a newsflash: *Sears won't be here in 15 years.*

As a young lad, I made countless trips to Sears with my father to buy tools, paint, and appliances, and continued that tradition into my adulthood. Comedian Tim Allen joked often about his obsession with tools from Sears.

Sears used to be a *big* deal. What happened?

The Sears empire originated in 1886, when Richard Sears, a railroad agent in small-town Minnesota, began selling surplus watches, at a handsome profit, to his fellow station agents. He then used various mail-order catalogs to move his merchandise. To grow, he relocated to Chicago, where he met Alvah Roebuck, with whom he formed a partnership.

Together, Sears and Roebuck propelled their venture by publishing their own watch catalog, in 1888.

They diversified beyond watches by targeting rural farmers, who were limited to local general stores for acquiring their supplies. By 1894, the new Sears, Roebuck & Company was selling bikes, sporting goods, cars, sewing machines, and other dry goods, via a 300-page catalog.

The catalog grew to over 500 pages a few years later by adding groceries, stoves, dolls, drugs, furniture, hardware, and almost everything farmers needed. Sears was the Amazon of its day.

The 1907 letterhead logo below screams *infrastructure and operations*, planting the seed of eventual destruction.

SEARS, ROEBUCK & CO.

WE SELL EVERYTHING BY MAIL ORDER ONLY. YOUR MONEY WILL BE PROMPTLY RETURNED FOR ANY GOODS NOT PERFECTLY SATISFACTORY AND WE WILL PAY FREIGHT OR EXPRESS CHARGES BOTH WAYS

OUR 40 ACRE NEW HOME - THE LARGEST MERCANTILE PLANT IN THE WORLD

BOUNDARIES: KEDZIE AVE. HARVARD ST. CENTRAL PARK AVE. AND CHICAGO TERMINAL TRANSFER R.R.

CABLE ADDRESS: SUPPLY CHICAGO. DIRECT WIRE WITH WESTERN UNION. AND POSTAL TELEGRAPH CO'S. LONG DISTANCE PHONE KEDZIE 2500. WITH PRIVATE EXCHANGE TO ALL DEPARTMENTS.

OUR MAMMOTH CATALOGUE CONTAINS OVER 100.000 ILLUSTRATIONS AND QUOTATIONS MAILED TO ANY ADDRESS FREE ON APPLICATION. THIS BIG BOOK NAMES THE LOWEST PRICES ON EVERYTHING WRITE FOR IT TODAY. WE CAN SAVE YOU MONEY ON ANYTHING YOU WANT TO BUY.

REFERENCE BY SPECIAL PERMISSION. FIRST NATIONAL BANK CHICAGO. CORN EXCHANGE NAT'L BANK CHICAGO. NATIONAL CITY BANK NEW YORK. NATIONAL SHAWMUT BANK, BOSTON.

That logo was a metaphor for the corporate DNA and brand. When a company like Sears changes an industry and has no real competition for several years, it can be whatever it wants to be, act any way it chooses to act. Customers have no choice but to tolerate all of it.

Complacency and Arrogance

Unchallenged success makes top executives feel cozy. Complacency and arrogance dominate the culture. The mirror of hubris replaces the window of opportunity. Changes in the terrain require accompanying changes in the company. But, middle managers fear challenging the DNA and the top execs. The brand suffers, and the dire destiny is then sealed.

Eventually, Roebuck left the company, which, in 1906, became the first retailer to go public. Richard Sears retired in 1908, replaced by Julius Rosenwald.

In 1925, Sears opened its first store, catering to men *and* women (a first), expanding beyond farms into cities, while continuing to build its mail-order-catalog business.

The Sears catalog had become known in retail circles as the "Consumers' Bible." In 1933, Sears published its first Christmas catalog, called the "Sears Wishbook," a winner.

Sears was a trendsetter on fire. But, the behemoth started resting on its laurels, believing in its own invincibility, and assuming the party would last. It didn't. Success always invites competition, which grants customers new and better options. Stasis shrinks margins and slows growth.

That's when Sears should have doubled down, to reassess its audience, organization, and terrain, to fine-tune its brand, to focus on its destiny—*not to get distracted.*

Even though it faced increasing competition from Lowes, Home Depot, Midas, Meineke, Firestone, Goodyear, Les Schwab, Best Buy, Costco, Walmart, Jiffy Lube, and many others, Sears didn't materially and forcefully respond.

All relationships—personal, professional, commercial, marital, and political—are based on awareness and growth. If they turn stagnant, they die.

This happened at Sears. Its stores grew outdated. Product quality suffered. Customer service tanked. Customers began asking themselves why they needed to shop at Sears. They defected in droves.

Starting in the 1930s, Sears unwisely diversified into insurance (Allstate), securities brokerage (Dean Witter), credit (Discover Card), real-estate brokerage (Coldwell Banker), mall development (Homart Development Company), online services (Prodigy), and home improvement (Orchard Supply Hardware).

Conglomeration is a *huge* red flag: it always fails.

First, it means the CEO can't fix his flagging business and instead acquires unrelated lines to mask that weakness. Eventually, profits sink further, the truth emerges, and the conglomerate is forced to divest the distractions.

Second, investors prefer pureplays. They can diversify their own portfolios—easily, quickly, and in ways befitting their risk profiles—and, therefore, don't need or want CEOs to do it for them by ineffectively conglomerating. But, to the untrained investor and journalist, conglomeration gives the magnificent appearance, *temporarily*, of a CEO's strategic brilliance and activity.

In 1974, Sears occupied its new HQ, the Sears Tower, then the world's tallest building. But, because of sinking fortunes—*in 1992, it lost $2.3B and cut 47,000 jobs; in 1993, it stopped publishing its catalog*—Sears was forced to sell its Tower in 1994. How symbolic of a meteoric rise and fall.

The Ed Lampert Era

In 2004, Kmart, another troubled retailer, purchased Sears, forming Sears Holdings. Ed Lampert, the CEO and chairman, has thrown lots of food against the wall to see what might stick: he frequently injected capital and sold Sears products through Costco and Ace Hardware. Nothing worked.

Sears Holdings, the union of Kmart + Sears, reminds me of a line from *Back to School,* the 1986 hit movie, in which Thornton Melon (Rodney Dangerfield) described his failed marriage: "We were doomed from the start. I'm an earth sign. She's a water sign. Together, we made mud."

Mud is right. Since 2006, revenues and net income have been declining. Moody's has determined that Sears needs a $1.5B infusion to survive 2017. Because Sears has no brand, no sensible destiny, and a disastrous bottom line, such an infusion would be a colossal waste of cash.

SEARS IS LOSING MONEY AS SALES TUMBLE

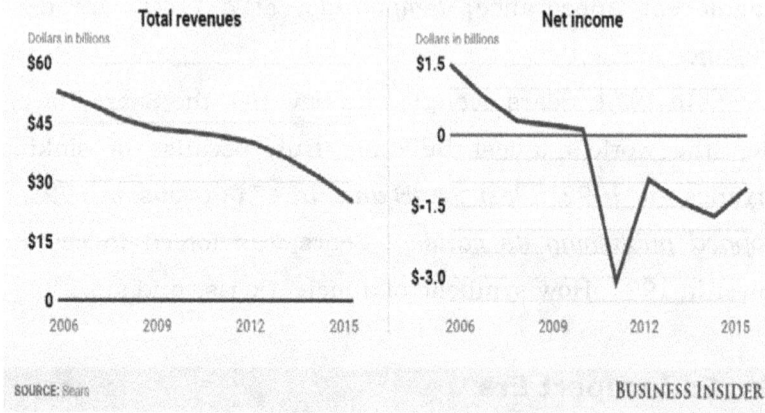

Total revenues

Dollars in billions

$60

$45

$30

$15

0

2006   2009   2012   2015

Net income

Dollars in billions

$1.5

0

$-1.5

$-3.0

2006   2009   2012   2015

SOURCE: Sears

BUSINESS INSIDER

According to a scathing article in *Business Insider*, on 01.08.17, by Haley Peterson, Ed Lampert is an absentee CEO, appearing in meetings only via video screen, inducing fear when he does. Here are excerpts from a 2015 videoconference, in which 12 employees were warned not to utter "consumer."

> *"He looks at the presenters and says, 'Do not say these words to that guy,'" according to a former Sears executive who described the meeting to Business Insider. "That guy" meant Lampert, who would soon appear on a giant projector screen at the front of the room, beamed in live from a home office inside a $38 million Florida estate—1,400 miles away from headquarters.*

The pad with the three words was out of sight of Lampert's video feed. One of the words on it was "consumer."

The stakes were high. If any of those words were uttered in front of Lampert, the two presenters would "get shredded" by the CEO, whose frequent tirades had fostered a climate of fear among the company's most senior managers, said another person—this one a former vice president.

These two and other executives say "consumer" can trigger Lampert. He wants employees to instead refer to shoppers as "members," which is his term for customers who are enrolled in Sears' Shop Your Way rewards program.

It was at that moment, as the executive attending the meeting watched fellow employees anxiously censor themselves in front of Lampert, that he realized he needed to flee the sinking 123-year-old company.

Bottom Line

When one contracts a disease, he must address it immediately—or it will irreversibly fester, and he'll die. Such is the dismal destiny of Sears: *predictable and preventable.*

While selling Craftsman and other labels, Sears is now reduced to monetizing its real estate—by closing stores and renting vacated spaces at competitive rates. In fact, mall owners want Sears to do just that. Moreover, Lampert, CEO of ESL Investments, which controls Sears and lends it money, personally benefits from Sears's downward spiral.

The Sears brand used to be consistency, affordability, reliability, quality, and dependability. Shoppers knew what they could expect and get at every store.

As competitors began to fill the landscape, Sears arrogantly lived off its legacy, took its eye off the ball, ignored its sinking brand and defecting customers, bought unrelated businesses, and let the world pass it by.

What a sad ending for an icon: *from leader to loser.*

Too often, CEOs know neither why they succeeded nor why they failed. When storm clouds arrive, they panic, blame the Internet, turn to financial gymnasts, and then sink.

Sears never moved beyond its *catalog mentality*—even in its stores. It didn't fathom branding, the changing terrain, and its avoidable decline. Instead, it stupidly diversified. It squandered time, money, and momentum

Learn from the needless demise of Sears, *regardless of your industry*. It's always brand, destiny, and bottom line.

CHAPTER FOURTEEN

Ratios & Formulas

Branding is as much art as science. It's not for data fanatics or for impractical, shoot-from-the-hip dreamers.

In the "GutShare" section of Chapter One, we reviewed the significance of emotions in purchasing and branding.

To excel at branding, the CEO, brander-in-chief, must value and prioritize it. Also, the CEO must be able to, and must hire those who are able to, do the following:

- Generally grasp human emotions and behaviors
- Identify target audience's emotions and behaviors
- Message audience's emotions back to the audience
- Verify and quantify messaging effectiveness.

There are ratios and formulas, proven over time, that help branders tap those emotions and behaviors, to convey to audiences the words, themes, sounds, and images, and combinations thereof, that will resonate with said audiences.

That's why the CEO can't delegate or entrust branding to amateurs. Choices and arrangements of messages matter in branding. Ignorance and apathy aren't excuses for failure.

The Vitruvian Man

Our first ratio example is the Vitruvian Man, which Leonardo da Vinci drew in 1490, based on the principles of Marcus Vitruvius Pollio, a Roman architect (died c. 15 BCE).

The Vitruvian Man stands inside a circle and a square, in two superimposed positions, with arms and legs apart. It was to be architecture's prime model of proportion. A guiding principle: the ideal body should be eight heads high.

Proportion determines the degree of attraction to an image and is, for example, a key factor in winning a beauty contest or a bodybuilding competition.

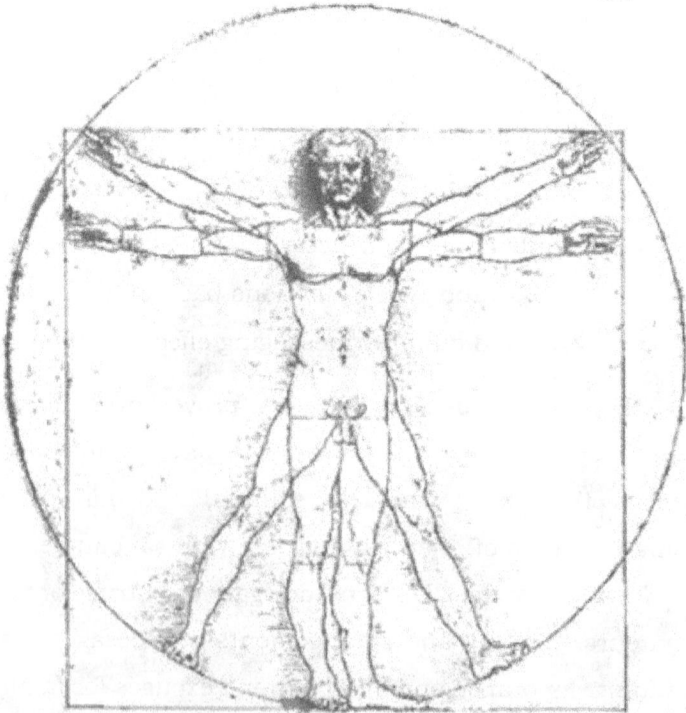

The Golden Ratio

The Golden Ratio (GR) is a mathematical relationship where $a + b$ is to a, as a is to b—and equals 1.618. It's based on the Fibonacci sequence (0, 1, 1, 2, 3, 5, 8, 13, 21, etc., where each number is the sum of the two preceding ones). To honor Phidias, who used the GR to make the Parthenon's statues, the Greek letter "Phi" represents it.

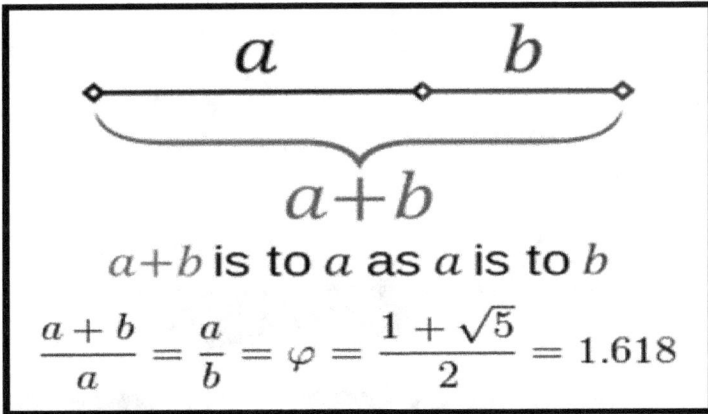

$$a \qquad b$$

$$a+b$$

$a+b$ is to a as a is to b

$$\frac{a+b}{a} = \frac{a}{b} = \varphi = \frac{1+\sqrt{5}}{2} = 1.618$$

The GR is prominent in all of nature, defining what is aesthetically pleasing to human emotions. Designers use the GR in logo design; architects use it to design buildings.

It turns out that beauty is *not* in the eye of the beholder but is formulaic, unbeknownst to most of us.

In the most-beautiful smiles, central incisors (front teeth) are 1.618X wider than the lateral incisors, which are 1.618X wider than canines, and so on.

Starting in 1677, Antonio Stradivari incorporated the GR in his iconic violins, which are replete with specific GR proportions, covering the upper and lower bouts, the waist, the neck, and the pegbox. The Golden Ratio and exquisite craftsmanship make it impossible for anyone to look away from a Stradivarius violin while in its presence.

Golden Ratio in Violins

$$\frac{a1 + a2}{a2} = \frac{a2}{a1} = \frac{b2}{b1} = \frac{b2}{c2} = \frac{c2}{c1} = \Phi$$

Brand Is Destiny.com

Other examples of GR's use include the Parthenon, as mentioned previously, the Porch of Maidens on the Acropolis, the Great Pyramid of Giza, and the Taj Mahal in India.

The Magic of Music

Like poetry, music has a structure. Songs have verses and refrains. Most symphonies have been written in three or four movements, usually in a fast-slow-fast format.

Why do certain songs grab us, make us cry? Adele's hit, "Someone Like You," is known to bring people to tears. Is it her lyrics? Perhaps. But, it's more than that.

Adele uses a musical device called an *appoggiatura*, an accented dissonance returning to consonance (low-to-high or high-to-low), modulating the pitch, creating a feeling of tension-release. When Adele sings the word "you" and others throughout the song, she briefly dips down to a discordant note and quickly returns to the original. Research shows that this technique, also used in instrumental and orchestral music, consistently grabs people's emotions.

In her piece in the *Wall Street Journal*, on 02.11.12, "Anatomy of a Tear-Jerker," Michaeleen Doucleff explains:

> When the music suddenly breaks from its expected pattern, our sympathetic nervous system goes on high alert; our hearts race, and we start to sweat. Depending on the context, we interpret this state of arousal as positive or negative, happy or sad.

The point is that music, written and performed in a specific way, universally affects us. We may not all cry, but we *react* to, *remember*, and *repeat* the notes and lyrics.

The Sitcom Formula

You may not realize it, but sitcoms adhere to a proven formula. Larry David (*Seinfeld, Curb Your Enthusiasm*) and Chuck Lorre (*Two and a Half Men, The Big Bang Theory*), two sitcom kings, have built fortunes on this formula.

A half-hour sitcom, minus commercials, is 22 minutes long. Each episode begins with the protagonist stating a goal or problem to be solved, and viewers hope that will happen by the end of the episode.

The first solution attempt usually hits a snag, forcing a new angle. Before the episode's end, the protagonist may or may not prevail, but viewers don't mind: They don't want their favorite characters to grow or change too much, unlike in movies, or they'll lose interest in watching every week.

According to Noah Charney's piece in the *Atlantic*, "The Sitcom Code," on 12.28.14, each episode unfolds this way:

Minutes 1-3: Teaser setup sketch before the credits

Minutes 3-8: Statement of problem or goal

Minutes 8-13: Solution execution hits snag (subplot)

Minutes 13-18: Protagonist succeeds or fails

Minutes 19-21: Outro, credits, life hasn't changed.

The point here is: creators of successful sitcoms use a *proven formula* to spark and retain emotional connections with audiences. *Ignore human psychology at your peril.*

CHAPTER FIFTEEN

Skip the Super Bowl

Notwithstanding my advice in the previous chapter, about ratios and formulas, you cannot be indiscriminate with your employment of emotion. The best example of this is advertising during the Super Bowl, a huge waste of money.

Recall the Monday after Super Bowl XLVIII, in 2014. Aside from Denver's humiliating loss, what was everybody talking and tweeting about? The winner of the "Commercial Bowl": Budweiser. It had run a spot featuring a puppy and a horse in an improbable lovefest. America swooned.

First, horses and dogs hate each other; the premise is silly. Second, this spot didn't sell any beer—the whole point of advertising. Anheuser-Busch/Inbev wasted $8 million per minute for the airtime, plus conception and production costs.

In the 2015 Super Bowl, Bud repeated that puppy-horse theme, with its "Lost Dog" spot, paying the new ad rate of $9 million per minute. Once again, Bud was the favorite.

Newsflash: Puppies don't sell beer!

This "Puppy Love" spot is redolent of Coca-Cola's Mean Joe Greene ad from 1980. *Everybody* loved it, too. It made people cry. It won awards. But, according to Sergio Zyman, Coca-Cola's then-CMO, this tearjerking, award-winning, beloved spot *didn't sell one bottle of Coke*—so he killed it. That's right: it failed. Pundits were shocked.

Advertising is *not* meant to be entertainment. It can be entertain*ing*—but not entertain*ment*. A commercial is a means to an end, *not* an end, *not* the object of awards. A commercial is a branding and sales vehicle. It has *one* job: *to persuade target customers to buy the product.* Period.

Evidence abounds, via study after study, that Super Bowl spots *don't* sell products. But, top companies—pushed by their CEOs—continue illogically throwing wasted cash at them. Why? Bragging rights. They become cool hipsters.

In 2010, Nielsen reported that *51 percent* of viewers prefer the Super Bowl commercials to the game itself. This means that the spots are entertain*ment*, a disaster.

At the typical Super Bowl party, people are talking, laughing, joking, yelling, drinking, eating, cheering, expecting to be entertained—*not paying attention to your brand.*

According to *USA Today's* Ad Meter, Budweiser has won the coveted "best commercial" slot for 13 of the last 16 Super Bowls, through 2016. Big deal. How's that working out?

From 2004 to 2013, the per-capita consumption of Budweiser fell 40 percent, from 30 cans to just 18 cans per year. Between 2007 and 2012, Beer sales, in general, were down 2.8%. Awards and accolades notwithstanding, Super Bowl advertising doesn't sell.

Would you send your best salesrep to a customer site to sing and dance, to recite Hamlet, or perform a comedy routine—then walk away? Would you? Doubtful. That's your Super Bowl commercial.

Would you send your best salesrep into a loud, crowded party to try to get an order? Doubly doubtful. That's your Super Bowl commercial.

Would you give your best salesrep an award for making customers cry but not getting them to buy? That's your Super Bowl commercial.

Notable anomaly: Apple's "1984" spot, which aired on January 22, 1984, during Super Bowl XVIII, to introduce the MacIntosh computer. Invoking themes and images of George Orwell's dystopian *1984,* a female athlete, who represented the new Mac and nonconformity itself, threw a long-handled sledgehammer at and through a giant video screen, depicting Big Brother (IBM). This spot—which Chiat/Day produced, Ridley Scott directed, and only Steve Jobs liked—almost didn't air. But, it did—*and sold $155M worth of Macs in the following 90 days.* Again, commercials must *sell,* not entertain.

Recall that, in 1984, there was no Internet and no smartphone and no Facebook. Cable TV was in its infancy. It was easy, then, to punch undistracted viewers in their guts with a bold, unique, memorable, challenging message during the Super Bowl. That ship has sailed.

Remember: If commercials make people laugh or make them cry, here's what they won't do: *make them buy.* Your job is to sell, *not to win awards.*

Leverage customers' emotions judiciously, to reinforce your company's brand, to sell, not to distract. If you waste the cash of shareholders, you'll make *them* cry.

CHAPTER SIXTEEN

Branding Execution

Understanding, valuing, and prioritizing branding is central to its success. Of course, good intentions can crash in the face of faulty execution, as in all endeavors.

HP Invent

I wrote about the branding challenges of Hewlett-Packard (HP), which recently split into two companies, in Chapter Nine of *Be Unique or Be Ignored.*

In September 2015, Meg Whitman, then CEO of HP and subsequently CEO of HP Enterprise (one of the after-split entities), announced that she would terminate 30K employees, 10% of its workforce, to save $2.7B annually.

Most of the departing 30,000 staffers came from HP's IT-outsourcing business—a remnant of the exorbitantly priced $13.9B purchase of EDS in 2008. Unfortunately for HP, EDS was in a shrinking industry. Oops.

Bolting together billion-dollar companies can jack up revenues, but rarely does it build customer *value.*

What happened? I'll give you a perspective that you'll likely read nowhere else.

Carly Fiorina, former presidential candidate in 2016, became CEO of HP in July 1999. Shortly after arriving in the C-suite, she rebranded the company, to invoke its startup roots, by inaugurating the "HP Invent" campaign. This action ultimately put HP on a path of unmanageable doom.

Imagine driving to work at HP every day, passing this odd *HP Invent* sign. You'd ask yourself, Invent *what?* For *whom?* What's the goal here? How do we execute *that?*

Invent is what research facilities do—not solutions companies. Fiorina made HP's brand indeterminate, pointing the behemoth toward a destructive destiny.

When a company's products and technologies trump or delete its brand, one can draw two simple conclusions: the CEO rejects branding; the firm will operate as an entroprise.

That happened to HP.

Branding is not just for customers, investors, and reporters; it's also for *employees*. If your troops don't know why their employer exists and why it's unique, they'll make lots of random, stupid, tactical decisions—*or none at all.*

Appledygook

In January 2017, Apple's board reduced CEO Tim Cook's pay by 15 percent for missing 2016's sales goals. In October 2016, Apple reported its first decline in annual sales (down 8 percent) and profits (down 14 percent) in 15 years.

Back in May 2016, Cook appeared with Jim Cramer, host of *Mad Money* on CNBC, to explain Apple's revenue and stock slump. He made an arrogantly disturbing remark, portending an avoidable branding suicide: *"We're going to give you things that you can't live without, that you just don't know you need today."*

First, customers don't need, and do not buy, "things." Second, lots of people are living without the Apple Watch, which Cook launched a year prior to CNBC's interview. Third, people know what they need today; they just don't know the possible solutions to what they need.

Imagine the impact on Apple's employees viewing Cook with Cramer. How would they execute on such Appledygook? What's the brand, the direction and purpose, the destiny?

I'll bet Mr. Cook hasn't recently called AppleCare, the customer-service hotline, or visited a Genius Bar, the in-store customer-service area. Rarely does one receive a pleasant experience in either venue. Customer experience is a major component of brand, as you'll see later in this chapter.

When Mr. Cook told Mr. Cramer, "We're going to give you things that you can't live without," my immediate reaction was: Who is *you*?

Apple's arrogance led it into the driverless-car biz and, as reported widely on January 12, 2017, into making original movies and TV shows, competing with Netflix and Amazon. Imagine what the employees are thinking as they try to describe Apple, even to themselves.

Peter Thiel, investor and cofounder of PayPal, told Maureen Dowd of the *New York Times*: "We know what a smartphone looks like and does. It's not the fault of Tim Cook, but it's not an area where there will be any more innovation."

Robert Hackett, of *Fortune*, backed Thiel's assessment: "Despite Thiel's reputation as an avowed contrarian, his argument that the tech giant will struggle to innovate beyond the iPhone-as-we-know-it is not exactly unconventional. Amid slipping sales, analysts have voiced concerns that Apple, whose market cap exceeds $600 billion, has no 'next big thing' in sight to combat declines in revenue growth."

A product-centric company always needs a *next-big-thing* innovation to maintain its momentum and bottom line. By contrast, a brand-centric company continuously monitors its customers' needs and wants, and seamlessly supplies the "right" products and services, at the right times.

An all-over-the-map vendor like Apple can't define its target customer, because it has none. It hubristically believes it can live off its legacy, possessing the power and magic to satisfy *everyone*, with every product and service, at all times, despite having strong, hungry rivals and no definable destiny.

Unify Your Pitch

When dealing with almost every company, we learn invariably that the proverbial right and left hands have never met and are unlikely to do so any time soon. This repulses us.

Such is true at electrical utilities, phone and cable companies, government agencies, retailers, large corporations, and fledgling startups—entroprises all.

Why so much dysfunction?

People, in general, are narcissistic, directionless, and poor communicators. They behave randomly.

Surprisingly, many CEOs are either unaware of or in denial about the organizational dysfunction in their ranks. Why else would it exist and persist?

As often as possible, when speaking to groups of CEOs, I pose this challenge: *Query your employees about how they describe your company to each other and outsiders. What would they say?* I usually get crickets and awkwardness.

Why?

Branding is not a priority—nor is unity, preparation, and discipline. Recall what Tim Cook told Jim Cramer (above). Employees emulate the CEO.

Problem: When employees are confused and in the dark, outsiders are worse-off. Dysfunction is expensive.

Such confusion compounds when each employee, without guidance, pitches a different message to the five key constituent groups: *customers, investors, partners, reporters, and analysts (financial and industry)*. Sadly, this is the rule, not the exception.

Constituent groups are, unfortunately, accustomed to getting conflicting pitches from your company's homepage, brochures, advertising, news releases, tradeshows, keynotes, media interviews, and public-facing employees. Think again about the left-hand-right-hand problem.

As we discussed in the "Fear of Branding" section of Chapter Eight, you run the risk of creating a Tower of Babel when your corporate pitch and employees aren't unified.

So, what *should* your company's "pitch" be?

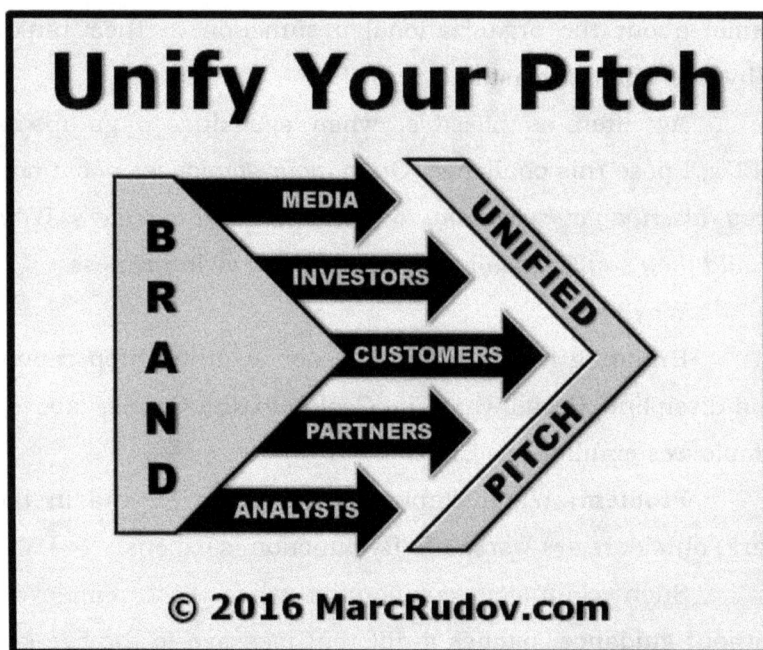

Your pitch is, quite simply, your brand: your unique, customer-validated value proposition. That means *all* pitches are customer-centric, *articulated in customer language*: no product, technology, company, or industry jargon. All pitches are unified, slight variations on a theme, almost identical.

A person should be able to walk from a customer pitch to an investor pitch and *hear the same message.* Is this true at your company? I'm betting it's not.

Yes, the investor pitch will include financial metrics and timelines, but *its kernel must be the customer pitch.* That's why customers are in the center of the "unify" graphic above.

If the dogs aren't eating the dog food, financial metrics are worthless—and high-caliber investors know that.

An investor challenged me in one of my presentations: *"You're wrong. We must use the jargon Wall Street tells us to use."* My reply: "BS. Where does Wall Street get that jargon? From geeks in Silicon Valley. *You* tell Wall Street what to say."

If your company hasn't earned customer validation for its brand, and you *prematurely* seek the blessings of analysts and the capital of investors, you'll have *no leverage* to create your brand, your pitch—*and not be in control of your destiny.*

Instead, *investors* will dictate your pitch—according to *their* buzzwords—and you'll blend in with your jargon-spewing competitors. This is *branding failure.* Never allow it.

Unify your pitch and your employees, each of whom must be able to recite, in his sleep, with identical words, why your company exists and how it's unique. No winging it.

The key here is to test your employees. Can they recite your brand, your pitch? If not, why not? Remedy this, ASAP.

Every constituent pitch—customer, investor, partner, media, analyst—whether written or verbal, should be virtually identical and expressed on *your* terms, not Wall Street's or your industry's terms. Micromanage and enforce this, or else risk chaos and obscurity.

Message Trumps Megaphone

I touched on this topic in my previous book but will reemphasize it here. Branding has two components: message and megaphone. *Message* trumps megaphone. When most people hear branding, they think *megaphone*—a big reason they claim, incorrectly, that they're "not ready" for it.

What Is Branding?
Message + Megaphone
MESSAGE TRUMPS MEGAPHONE

MURKY MESSAGE

© 2016 MarcRudov.com

Anyone can step up to a megaphone, but that doesn't mean he has anything valuable to say or is a good speaker. In fact, if you have nothing to say, a megaphone is your worst enemy!

A megaphone can be a microphone in front of a live audience, radio, TV, newspaper, homepage, social media, etc. Without a strong message, the audience will not *react* to, *remember*, and *repeat* it (see "Brand Essentials" in Chapter One).

If one conveys a murky, jargon-filled message through a megaphone, he gets a *louder* jargon-filled, murky message out the other side.

If you use jargon, your company is generic, not unique—and, thus, it has no message and no brand.

The megaphone is the easy part of branding. The message is the tough part of branding—and that's why it's rarely done well, if at all.

This is why *message* trumps megaphone, why it *must* be developed skillfully *on the first day of a company's life—* before products, customers, employees, and revenues. Finally, you must verify your message's effectiveness by testing it on real human beings, in person.

Zero-Based Branding™

You're likely familiar with zero-based budgeting, the system of forcing execs to justify every line item's existence, every year, rather than presume it should remain in the budget.

Employ the same practice for your products, every year, where each one must fit your company's *brand*. I call this practice Zero-Based Branding™.

Put every one of your company's products under the brand's magnifying glass. *Never presume it should live.*

If you cannot brand-justify any product, modify it accordingly—or scrap it altogether. *Of course, to do this, you must first have a strong brand.*

In 1869, Louis Sullivan, the Boston-born "father of skyscrapers," asserted that *form follows function.* Function is purpose. All successful designers follow Sullivan's axiom.

Unsuccessful designers build products based on love of technology, with no regard for or knowledge of who will benefit from and purchase said products—*and why.*

Newsflash: If you don't know a product's purpose—the problem it solves or wish it grants—you can't determine its shape, its physical configuration, and its form.

How, then, does one determine function? Simple: *brand begets function*. Hence, zero-based branding.

Yet, as I've indicated previously, I hear this refrain from CEOs, time after time: *We'll develop our product first and worry about the branding later.* They think branding is mere fluff, wrapping paper—instead of the blueprint, the bedrock of product development and customer experience. They think brand follows form, and they are mistaken.

To wit: Every patent is, theoretically, a unique product or would-be product. Each one, therefore, *should* be a smashing commercial success, right? Wrong. According to a June 18, 2014, article in *Forbes* magazine:

> *Of today's 2.1M active patents, 95 percent fail to be licensed or commercialized. These unlicensed patents include over 50K high-quality patented inventions developed by universities. More than $5T has been spent in the US alone on research and development over the past 20 years, much of which went to create the very patents that remain unlicensed. According to Forrester Research, "US firms annually waste $1T in underused intellectual property assets by failing to extract the full value of that property through partnerships." In other words, we're pouring money—and productivity—down the drain.*

Lesson: A unique product is *meaningless* unless customers, potential and actual, value it. How do you know whether they value it? With skillful branding— begun *before* the product is conceived or built. I'll repeat that: begun *before* the product is conceived or built.

Put another way: Treat products as employees; don't "hire" them *unless they fit your brand.*

Awareness Is Not Your Goal

CEOs frequently ask me how to increase awareness, specifically brand awareness. My usual response: *Increasing awareness is not your goal and is a total waste of money.*

Other than establishing bragging rights and scratching the entertainer itch, the stated motive for ill-fated advertising in the Super Bowl is: *We're trying to increase awareness.*

Branding is *not* about building awareness—it's about *creating emotional connections* with customers in all business sectors: military, industrial, commercial, financial, medical, and consumer.

AWARENESS IS *NOT* YOUR GOAL
MarcRudov.com

Researchers at Oregon State University determined that only 2.7% of Americans live a healthy lifestyle. Certainly, the other 97.3% are *aware* of their negligent, self-destructive behaviors. So what? Awareness without action is useless.

Recall GutShare. There are *no* cerebral purchases. I'm aware of hundreds of companies and products, and I don't care about any of them. Why? They're in my head, instead of in my gut, where I and all other humans make purchase decisions.

The sole goal of branding is to magnetically attract customers with open wallets, ready to buy. You can do this only by offering them *value*—not giving them names to memorize, not making empty promises—and by concisely articulating that value in their language. But, the "eyeballs and impressions" crowd doesn't want to hear this.

I've heard many executives say, delusionally, that branding oneself merely entails appearing and speaking in some forum. If that were true, Jeb Bush would have demolished Donald Trump.

Without a gut-level connection to your customers, you have no brand—*despite your awareness quotient.* A strong brand begets attraction and action; being "known" does not.

PR Is Not Branding

It's common for a CEO to hear the word "branding" and think, This is a job for my public-relations (PR) team.

Mistake: PR is *not* branding.

Branding sets your company's direction and purpose—its destiny—and specifies its products, people, and processes.

PR is the art of getting *free publicity* by spinning *tactical* objectives—spreading the word about new products or controlling the damage from mishaps.

Newsflash: Not only is PR not branding, but, when its practitioners act like printing presses, it isn't PR, either.

To wit: Many companies continuously issue slews of utterly boring news releases about their latest products, believing they constitute news. They don't. Good reporters will ignore them.

Every now and then, though, a stellar exemplar emerges.

When Tylenol experienced its poisoning crisis in 1982, Johnson & Johnson, its parent firm, used PR and rapid response to maintain the public's trust, *which it had earned previously with top-notch branding.* Customers always had deemed Tylenol the safe choice for relieving pain, despite buying a commodity: acetaminophen.

Tylenol proved that success in PR depends on timing, reputation, and message—not volume. The question is, *What message?*

PR Is *NOT* Branding

P/R

DON'T BE CONFUSED

BRAND

© 2016 MarcRudov.com

Branding, unlike PR, is neither contemporaneous nor tactical. Its goal is to put your ship on a sustainable long-term course—its destiny—to articulate to target audiences why your firm exists and why it's unique, *not* to spin a crisis and *not* to get free publicity.

But, a strong brand can help get that free publicity.

The brand is ink and PR the quill. PR professionals, AKA flacks, must draw from the brand—created by branding experts—by religiously dipping their quills in it. Consequently, they'll come across to the outside world as consistent and coordinated.

Warning: It's *not* the job of flacks—nor is it in their expertise—to create your brand. So, expecting or requiring them to do so is a recipe for disaster.

If your company has a weak brand—or none at all— flacks, like salesreps, will invent your message as they go along. Worse, what they write will be product-centric and jargon-filled, thereby violating the premise of branding.

I've hired many flacks in my career—and fired them, usually for poor writing skills. Like a hawk, I always had to micromanage them. The more tools I gave them, such as a full inkwell, the better they performed. But, I spent too much time rewriting their grammatically incorrect news releases.

Note: *Because of texting and social media, excellent writing and speaking skills, and branding expertise, are now rarer than at any time in history.*

PR is not branding. Branding is not PR. Flacks are not branders. Keep that inkwell full and relevant. If your ship is adrift, PR is not your problem or your solution.

Hacking Company Growth

Unless you dwell in a cave, you've noticed that the buzzword "growth-hacking" is omnipresent in daily business chatter, as well as in articles, books, and seminars.

This buzzword is counterproductive.

Newsflash: Hack, as a noun and a verb, has a *negative* connotation. Growth-hacking, therefore, is both oxymoronic and moronic.

Regrettably, words don't matter in technology circles, where growth-hacking originated in 2010. We see the same disregard with the words "market" and "brand."

When communicating compellingly and memorably to customers, investors, reporters, and employees—also known as branding—words are paramount.

Words do matter.

Confusion and ambiguity are anathema to branding. Using any word or phrase that is not crystal-clear and unique will hurt your brand and, therefore, your bottom line.

Yet, confusion and ambiguity reign in business— unnecessarily spiking the costs of sales, capital, and media.

Let's review the definitions of hack and hacking:

A hack is an incompetent person, pretending to excel.

One who cannot cope with a situation "can't hack it."

Hacking is the act of cutting or destroying people and property, as well as invading a safe or a computer.

So, to s-t-r-e-t-c-h the definition of hacking to also mean creatively growing one's company, on a small budget, using every megaphone imaginable, makes zero sense. *Stop it.*

Words do matter.

There's a solution and word already on the shelf for expanding one's company: *branding.* No negative connotation or double-meaning. It's neither confusing nor ambiguous.

Alas, too many CEOs, such as the former Wells Fargo CEO, John Stumpf, have dismissed branding—and paid high prices for doing so. In fact, John Stumpf literally hacked his company's growth (killed it) by sullying its reputation.

One cannot develop a winning message without viscerally understanding his customers—impossible by relying on social media. Only a hack would pump impotent messages through all conceivable megaphones. Sadly, hacks abound.

Make branding your #1 priority, never put a hack in charge of it, and don't be a hack. Fire all executives who "can't hack it" in fixing your company's brand. Brand your company to impressive growth—or hack it to death, as Sears did.

Customer Experience

I'm amused at all the declarations of devotion, of late, to customer service and customer experience.

Like just discovering that water flows downhill, CEOs are now realizing that taking care of customers is good for business. Maybe they're sick of seminars about supply-chain management and continuous improvement.

Here's the real reason: most companies are product-centric. So, customer service, to them, is an extracurricular, detached entity—and it shows. It's a cleanup department for shortcomings and mistakes.

There's a professional group called the Customer Experience Board that helps CMOs deal with such issues. Why isn't this common sense?

In a brand-centric firm, however, customer service is inherent in its product offering. A brand-centric company promotes its brand, not its products and tools. Customers buy value, not products and tools, and expect to benefit from a resultant positive experience.

Here's a scene from an episode of *Frasier* ("Door Jam"; first aired: 01.07.03). It's uncannily perceptive in its treatment of *the customer experience*. Frasier Crane, played by Kelsey Grammer, arrives at La Porte D'Argent, a snooty upscale day spa, which purposely operates without signage. Proud to be breathing such rarified air, Frasier looks around for evidence he's in the right place, then approaches the receptionist:

Frasier: Hello. Uh, is this La Porte D'Argent?

Receptionist: Yes, it is.

Frasier: Ah, good. Say, someone was asking me earlier today about La Porte D'Argent, and I had a difficult time characterizing it. Uh, what would you tell him?

Receptionist: We try to discourage word of mouth.

Frasier: That's exactly what I said. So, oh, well, I'm here to take advantage of your offer.

Receptionist: Sure.

Frasier hands the receptionist the invitation.

Receptionist: Can I have your name, please?

Frasier: Yes, Frasier Crane.

The receptionist types on the computer.

Receptionist: I'm not finding you.

Frasier: Try Doctor Frasier Crane. Perhaps you've heard my popular radio show.

Receptionist: I'm not really a radio person. I'm sorry, Dr. Crane. You're not on the list. I can't let you in.

Frasier: But I have an invitation.

Receptionist: Yes, but you're not on the list.

Frasier: Yes, but I do have an invitation.

Receptionist: But, you aren't on the list.

Frasier: Yes, well, if I'm on the list, I wouldn't need an invitation, would I? I would just say that I'm on the list. Therefore, the invitation supersedes the list.

Receptionist: No, invitations are given out only to those on the list.

Frasier: Aha, but you do concede that I have a valid invitation?

Receptionist: Yes.

Frasier: Then it naturally follows that I would be on the list.

Receptionist: But you're not.

Frasier: Then how did I get the invitation?

Receptionist: I really don't know. You could have stolen it.

First, Frasier shyly admits he doesn't know how to characterize the spa—*evidence that, other than snootiness, it has no brand.* Then, the condescending receptionist sniffs that La Porte D'Argent prefers "pretentious" ambiguity.

This exchange reminds me of many encounters I've had with companies of all kinds, except brand-centric ones. If your company has the attitude and manner of La Porte D'Argent—whether intentionally or not—fix it, ASAP.

In 2015, Comcast and TimeWarner Cable were slated to combine in a $45B deal. But, because Comcast's "customer service" was so abhorrent, regulators nixed the merger. Circulating widely were shocking audioclips of Comcast's employees berating customers with invoice questions as well as those choosing to unsubscribe. In fact, a vendor called AirPaper sprung up to handle dealings with Comcast, on behalf of customers, for $5 per incident. Insane!

In response to this well-deserved public humiliation, Comcast initiated a punctuality policy, promising to credit customers' bills $20 every time the cable guy is late.

Why did Comcast let things devolve to that level?

It viewed the world through the prism of its network, instead of through its customers. Recall that we discussed this issue in the "Cordcutters" section of Chapter Three. It would have been easy to avoid this mess.

If your company has the pompous, disdainful attitude and manner of the shamed Comcast—whether intentionally or not—fix it, ASAP.

*A brand-centric company makes the positive customer experience **integral to its offering**, minimizing the need for a separate cleanup operation called customer service.*

Think about it. Nobody wants to deal with a customer-service department, an undesirable cost of ownership. Don't create one. Create a strong brand instead.

Salesreps Are Taxi Meters

The biggest complaint prospects and customers have about salesreps: they're unprepared. They show up on calls not knowing the customers (insulting), not knowing their own companies (embarrassing), while possessing inadequate or inappropriate collateral (unprofessional).

The average cost of a salescall, across all industries, is $600. And, it often takes five calls to close a sale. That's three grand per sale.

Talk is expensive, especially when it's ineffective and wastes time. Salesreps are taxi meters, and their meters are always running. What are you getting for your money?

SALESREPS ARE TAXI METERS
Time Is Money

02 TARIFF $48.50 FARE
$5.10 TOLLS $2.00 EXTRAS

AVERAGE SALESCALL $600

SALESREP PROSPECT

MarcRudov.com

Perhaps you can relate to this experience. I attended a medical-instrumentation tradeshow and visited the booth of one of the exhibitors. I spoke to the CEO:

> After initial small talk, he lamented about his biggest problem: *customers don't understand his product.* He asked whether I might know very technical people who could explain his product.
>
> I told him that he has the *opposite* problem: You need *less*-technical or *non*technical people who can explain the *value* of your offering, quickly, without diving into the weeds. Your current pitch is too long, too boring,

and too arcane. I'll bet you have to repeat it multiple times. He confirmed this.

I indicated that he was just describing the product's innards, *not its value*: You must articulate your firm's brand in 15 seconds, in *customer* language—*without* referring to your product or its technology, citing your SIC code, or uttering industry jargon—so customers will *react* to, *remember*, and *repeat* your message, *and buy your product*. If you won't do that, prospects often will say, "I'll think about it." *That* is your problem!

Instead, you just stated that your goal is to be *more* technical—which would drive down your price (and drive up your cost of sales). **What you say dictates** *what they pay*. The harder it is to understand you, the *less* they'll pay—*if they buy at all*.

When you have a strong brand, customers **promptly** grasp the value you offer them and identify with it— because you're using *their* language, expressing *their* pain. And, that's why "techies" are ill-suited for sales.

Despite agreeing intellectually, he recoiled emotionally, stubbornly digging in his heels, clinging to old ways and convictions. Clearly, he was butt-hurt from the exchange—typical for a product-centric firm's CEO.

Even good salespeople need direction. If your company has either no destiny or a nebulous one, I told him, salesreps won't know what to say. They'll invent their own jargon-laced pitches and show up unprepared. *They need a strong brand and proper training.*

Learn from this illustrative vignette, *regardless of your industry*. That CEO could have been you, and likely is.

There's no excuse for your salesreps to be unprepared in front of prospects and customers. It's unprofessional, and it hurts your company's reputation and, therefore, its brand.

When you're stuck in traffic, in a taxi, that meter's still running, costing you money. It's infuriating. Think about that anger and analogy every time you assess your salesreps.

But, if you brush aside your salesreps' lack of proper training, because of your weak brand, you are *minimizing* your shareholders' wealth.

And, please don't use the modern kneejerk panacea for poorly performing salesreps: *social media.* Unless you're Kim

Kardashian hocking jewelry or nudity, you *can't* sell anything via social media. **Fix your brand and train your salesreps.**

Your Cost of Customers

Do you know your cost of customers? Are you sure?

Most dialogue about customers hinges on two points: the cost of *acquiring* them and the products they buy. If this is the case in your company, sound the alarm.

First, thinking your company can "acquire" a customer is delusional—the epitome of hubris. It connotes *ownership*.

Newsflash: *You cannot and do not own customers; eliminate acquisition from your sales and marketing lexicon.*

Words beget attitudes, which beget behaviors. The very second a customer senses that a supplier views him as chattel—a la the cable-TV carriers—his resentment escalates and thoughts about defecting begin.

Second, equating product purchases with *customer demand* is myopic and amateurish. To reiterate earlier points: Customers demand and buy *value*, not products.

A product is merely the *current* fulfillment of a brand's promise; it's the brand's emissary. If your company has a weak brand or no brand, and is product-driven, **it'll bounce around like a pinball**—or a lost ship.

How to grasp and manage your cost of customers?

Know the customer and heed the true customer cycle, as depicted in the graphic below: identify the customer, then

172 ♦ Marc H. Rudov

enter the endless loop (for repeat business) of *convince,
engage, serve, satisfy,* and *verify.*

Each of these stages, and its outcome, is measurable—
in direct proportion to customer proximity. The more distant
and faceless your customers, the less you'll know them and
their cycle costs. It's common sense and explains Amazon's
recent foray into physical retail stores (see Chapter Four).

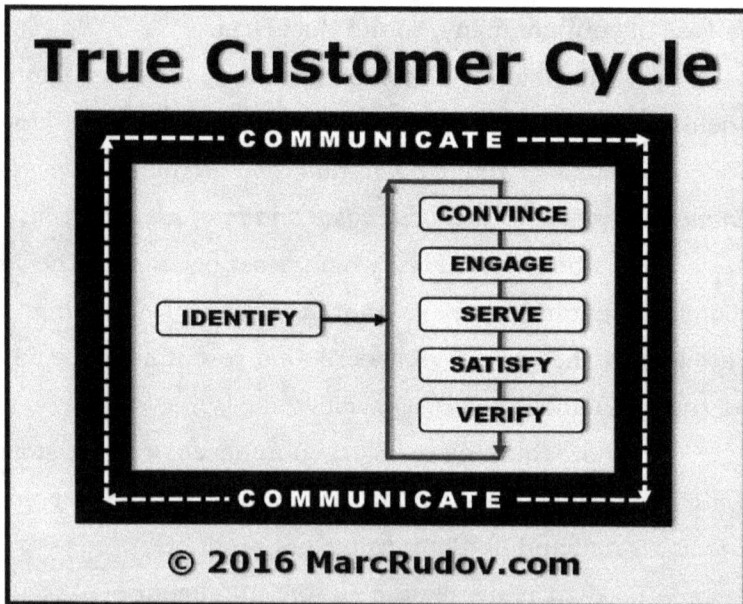

True Customer Cycle

COMMUNICATE

IDENTIFY

CONVINCE
ENGAGE
SERVE
SATISFY
VERIFY

COMMUNICATE

© 2016 MarcRudov.com

Two properties of the true customer cycle: it's bereft of
"acquire" and the "ownership attitude"; *convincing* is required
for every sale—no presumption.

NOTE: Identifying the ideal customer, the first step of
branding, is critical. In my experience, too many companies
don't have target customers; they're simply open for business.

Consequently, they don't know why customers buy, whether they're satisfied, or if they're profitable to serve.

Most important, the entire cycle is enveloped in a loop of constant communication—so that neither customers nor employees are in the dark, at any stage of the cycle.

Never put "I-text-I-don't-talk" staffers and contractors, *with no experience in face-to-face selling and a preference for clicks over humans*, in branding and marketing positions.

Finally, to cut your cost of customers, you must know that cost. That's possible only when you *know your customers, how you attracted them, and why they're still customers.*

How Branding Resembles Golf

Donald Trump almost blew the election: he ignored golf's basics. In golf, as in branding, there are three successive stages—the tee, the fairway, and the green—each requiring a different approach and tool.

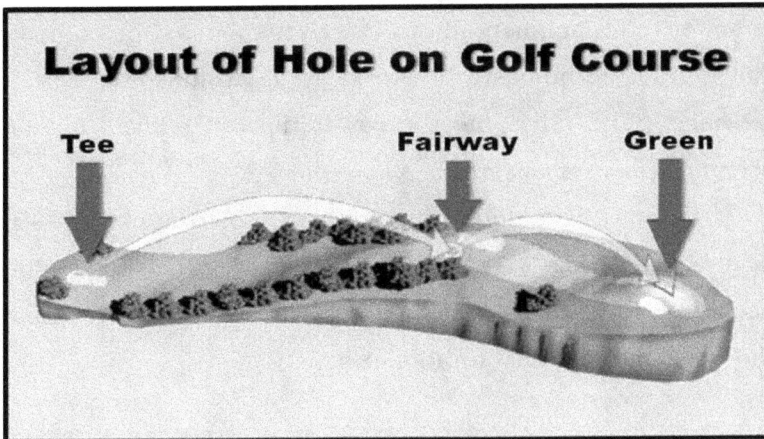

Layout of Hole on Golf Course

Tee   Fairway   Green

Hitting a ball from the tee, located hundreds of yards from the green, requires enormous power and control. From the fairway, strokes require less power and more finesse. Finally, sinking a putt on the green demands the least power and the most accuracy and finesse.

Using the wrong power and tool at each juncture—a putter on the tee (underpowered) or a driver on the green (overpowered)—will yield utter failure.

Before hiring Kellyanne Conway as his campaign manager, Trump responded thusly to massive criticism that he change his game by becoming less combative and more informed about policy matters: *I know what got me here; I'm not changing anything*—a common CEO refrain.

After Ms. Conway joined Trump's campaign, he heeded golf's basics with a drastic increase in discipline.

Golf is an apt metaphor for branding. In the beginning, a company must overcome competitive gravity and make waves to connect with potential customers—and it needs a lot of power to accomplish all of that. Over time, as the company moves from enthusiasts to tire-kickers, it must fine-tune its messaging and attenuate the power thereof, *without actually changing the core message.*

When Steve Jobs returned as CEO to Apple in 1997, he instituted the "Think Different" campaign, using famous people, dead and alive, to inspire new customers. It ignited the world and put IBM on its heels.

Today, Apple is not brusque and in your face with its messaging. If, however, Apple continues its revenues slide, or Samsung puts a huge dent in the company, or Apple suffers a massive product failure, it will have to remedy the issues and return to the tee for a branding reset.

If golf is not your game, there's another metaphor I like for making the same point: the three-stage rocket.

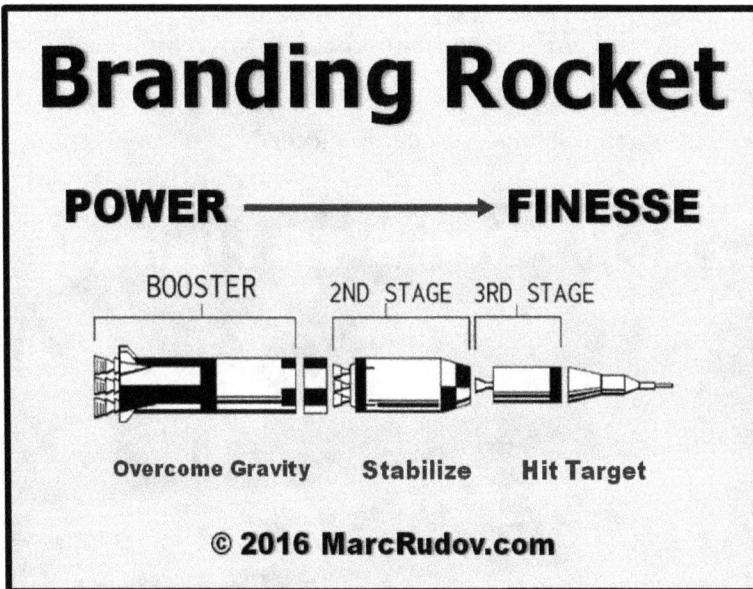

Branding Rocket

POWER ──────► FINESSE

BOOSTER   2ND STAGE   3RD STAGE

Overcome Gravity   Stabilize   Hit Target

© 2016 MarcRudov.com

The first stage is the largest and has maximum power. Its job is to overcome gravity. The second stage is smaller, has less power, and is charged with stabilizing the vehicle and refining course accuracy. Finally, the third stage is the smallest, has the least power and most finesse, and guides the payload to its target.

Obviously, by reversing the stages, the rocket would never get off the ground. And, if the third stage were as big and powerful as the first, the payload would overshoot and miss its target.

Whether you prefer the golf or rocket metaphor, the principle is identical: *Move from power to finesse as your level of emotional connection to the target customers increases.*

Never use too much or too little power, and always use the right tool. Again, without knowing your audience—*your customers*—your company, yourself, and where you are headed—*your destiny*—you can't succeed.

FROM POWER TO FINESSE

CHAPTER SEVENTEEN

The Ultimate Bottom Line

This book demonstrates, through axiomatic principles and numerous examples, that your company's brand fixes its destiny—and is the ultimate bottom line.

These correlations are true regardless of your industry or company size and age. In fact, branding begins on the *first* day of business—*before* you design a product or hire a staff.

If ever you should deem branding unimportant or delayable, beware: *failure is in your company's future.*

Branding is *not* an asterisk, an afterthought, an extra-curricular activity, or veneer. It *is* the *core* of your company, the *root* of its future, the *acorn* of its oak, the *blueprint* of its construction, the *itinerary* of its journey.

Recall the decline of Sears, the classical entroprise. Its brand faltered while clueless top executives watched it drift and uncontrollably bleed red ink. It went from leader to loser.

Use whatever travel metaphor you like: sea, land, or air. It matters not. *Without a strong brand, your firm will drift, spin, crash, and die.* Brand is destiny.

BRAND IS DESTINY™

The Ultimate Bottom Line

Brand Is Destiny.com

Only *you*, the CEO, can force your company to be brand-centric (vs. product-centric or technology-centric) by educating, leading, coaching, and rewarding your employees—and by *enforcing the rules of branding.*

Every member of your branding team—internal and external—*must follow these rules and employ a unified pitch.*

Without a strong grasp of and belief in branding, the CEO will dismiss it. He won't be able to spot the bullshitters and hacks, and won't know whether an incremental tweak or radical jolt is necessary to correct the company's course.

As CEO, you must know your terrain, your company, your audience, and yourself—and be immune to, and ready to fight, the distracting evil forces of political correctness.

Accordingly, don't hinge your destiny on the infantile behavior of snowflake Millennials, either as customers or employees. Branding requires maturity and accountability.

A healthy bottom line depends on success in *all* the revenue-based activities: sales, capital-raising, turnarounds, mergers & acquisitions, licensing, and business development. *And, branding is integral to every one of them.*

Be tough. Replace those who cannot or will not toe the branding line. Your branding team *must* comprise only those who eat, sleep, and drink solving customers' problems—*not sufferers of technologism and social-media addicts*—only those who are agnostic to predetermined "trendy" solutions.

Finally, without your imprimatur evident to *everyone* in the firm, branding will be little more than a "concept" your people casually and wrongly toss around—*and you will lose control of your destiny and bottom line.*

Bon voyage!

ABOUT THE AUTHOR

Marc Rudov is a branding advisor to CEOs, author of *Be Unique or Be Ignored: The CEO's Guide to Branding* and numerous articles, and a media commentator. He's headed marketing organizations in both large and small companies. Rudov is known worldwide as an independent thinker and thought-leader, unfazed by political correctness and technological correctness.

Mr. Rudov rails against industry, product, and technology jargon, and teaches his clients—from various industries—to escape their comfort zones to stand out, to be unique.

He counsels CEOs that, if they fail to lead and enforce their branding initiatives, they will create *entroprises*, imperil their destinies, and, consequently, squash their bottom lines.

Rudov earned his engineering degree from the University of Pittsburgh and his MBA from Boston University.

Marc Rudov is available for radio & TV appearances, debates, speaking engagements, and, of course, new clients. Find him at MarcRudov.com.